SALEM
Cornerstones of a Historic City

K. David Goss • "The Maritime History of Salem"

Richard B. Trask • "The Witchcraft Trials of 1692"

Bryant F. Tolles, Jr. • "The Historic Architecture of Salem"

Joseph Flibbert • "Nathaniel Hawthorne: Salem Personified"

Jim McAllister • "Salem Then and Now"

SALEM

Cornerstones of a Historic City

Joseph Flibbert • K. David Goss

Jim McAllister • Bryant F. Tolles, Jr.

Richard B. Trask

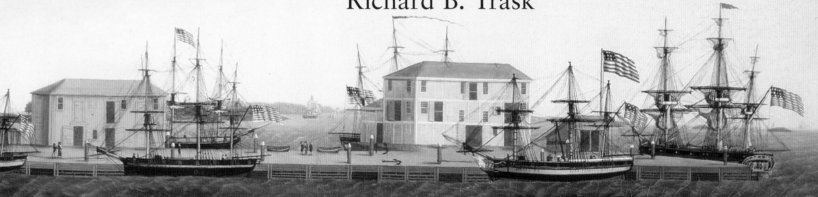

COMMONWEALTH EDITIONS

Beverly, Massachusetts

"The Maritime History of Salem" copyright © 1999 K. David Goss
"The Witchcraft Trials of 1692" copyright © 1999 Richard B. Trask
"The Historic Architecture of Salem" © 1999 Bryant F. Tolles, Jr.
"Nathaniel Hawthorne: Salem Personified" copyright © 1999 Joseph Flibbert
"Salem Then and Now" copyright © 1999 Jim McAllister

Library of Congress Cataloging-in-Publication Data
Salem : cornerstones of a historic city / Joseph Flibbert . . . [et al.].
    p. c.m.
    Includes bibliographical references and index.
    ISBN 1-889833-08-8 (cloth : alk. paper). -- ISBN 1-889833-09-6 (pbk. : alk. paper)
    1. Salem (Mass.)--History. 2. Historic sites--Massachusetts--Salem. 3. Salem (Mass.) Guidebooks.   I. Flibbert, Joseph.
F74.S1S27 1999
974.4'5--dc21
                                                                99-22398
                                                                CIP

Photo credits:
Front cover: The House of the Seven Gables (Ulrike Welsch)
Frontispiece: George Ropes, Jr., *Crowninshield Wharf* (Peabody Essex Museum)
Back cover: detail from *Friendship* by George Ropes, Jr. (Peabody Essex Museum); detail from *Examination of a Witch* by T. H. Matteson (Peabody Essex Museum); Charles Osgood portrait of Nathaniel Hawthorne (Peabody Essex Museum); Derby House (Mark Sexton)

Designed by Joyce Weston.
Published and distributed by Commonwealth Editions, an imprint of Memoirs Unlimited, Inc., 21 Lothrop Street, Beverly, Massachusetts 01915.
Printed in Hong Kong.

Contents

Chestnut Street. (Jim McAllister)

The Cornerstones of Salem

What makes a city historic? Dramatic events? Beautiful buildings? Famous men and women? In the case of Salem, Massachusetts, the answer is a combination of all these things. When residents, visitors, and students delve into Salem's history, they usually want to know more about one of four subjects:

- Salem's maritime history
- The witchcraft trials of 1692
- The historic architecture of Salem
- Nathaniel Hawthorne

These are the cornerstones of Salem's history. These are the principal subjects of this book.

Such an approach to Salem is not new. In 1988, Salem historian Jim McAllister said as much in the *New York Times*: "There are four reasons why people come to Salem—maritime history, architectural history, Nathaniel Hawthorne, and witches." More recently, William Story wrote *Touring Companion* and *Guide to the Four Historic Faces of Salem, Massachusetts*. That booklet's "faces" are this book's "cornerstones."

But until now, no book on Salem's historic high-lights has offered insightful articles by leading authorities, illustrated with color photographs of the city's great buildings and paintings.

How this book is organized

In *Salem: Cornerstones of a Historic City*, an all-star team of historians focuses on the four cornerstones, one at a time. Then McAllister, who also contributed the lion's share of the color photographs, explores Salem in the nineteenth and twentieth centuries, to understand what has been built on this diverse, fascinating foundation.

In chapter one, K. David Goss takes us back to Salem's earliest years as an English outpost. First settled by fishermen, Salem developed into one of the world's great trading ports by the end of the eighteenth century. Goss is an old Salem hand, having first worked at the Essex Institute in the 1980s. He moved on to become museum director of the House of the Seven Gables, a landmark that neatly represents all four cornerstones. Goss now serves as executive director of the historical society in neighboring Beverly, a town that was once part of Salem.

Richard B. Trask likewise lives and works in a former Salem district, Danvers, where he is the town archivist. Who better to write about the perplexing events of 1692, with that year's tragic trials and executions? Danvers, then known as Salem Village, was the site of the parish where the witch hysteria first took hold. Trask has devoted a good part of his career to understanding these events unique in American history, most recently in his book *The Devil Hath Been Raised: A Documentary History of the Salem Village Witchcraft Outbreak of March 1692.*

What has been raised in Salem over nearly four centuries of settlement has been one of the truly outstanding collections of American architecture. As former executive director of the Essex Institute, Bryant F. Tolles, Jr., was the author (with his wife, Carolyn K. Tolles) of the definitive work on the subject, *Architecture in Salem* (1983). That book is out of print, and Tolles has relocated to the University of Delaware, where he is a professor of history and art history and the director of the university's museum studies program. In *Salem: Cornerstones of a Historic City,* Tolles focuses on some of Salem's most significant homes and public buildings, and the people who built and lived in them.

Joseph Flibbert is a professor of English at Salem State College and a longtime contributor of articles and lectures on the author whose name is virtually synonymous with Salem, Nathaniel Hawthorne. In this book, Flibbert explains why Hawthorne, who lived no more than half his life in the city, may be viewed as Salem's representative man. Just as the four cornerstones are summed up in the Turner House, better known as the House of the Seven Gables, the first three cornerstones—maritime history, the witchcraft trials, and Salem architecture—are intimately associated with Hawthorne. Flibbert takes us into the author's life and most memorable writings to explore these themes.

Finally, Jim McAllister paints a detailed portrait of the city in the years since Hawthorne's death, demonstrating how the modern city has been built and rebuilt on its historic cornerstones. For fifteen years, McAllister has made Salem his study and passion, as an eloquent, insightful, and energetic teacher, lecturer, and guide. And he has often carried his camera with him, results of which are the many beautiful photographs he contributed to this book.

Salem has been blessed in recent years with at least two fine, dedicated photographers. The other is Mark Sexton of the Peabody Essex Museum. We are fortunate to have some of Sexton's photographs collected in this volume alongside McAllister's pictures, as well as photographs by Ulrike Welsch and Richard Trask and images from the archives of the Peabody Essex Museum, the House of the Seven Gables, the Danvers Archival Center, and the Beverly Historical Society.

Others who contributed to *Salem: Cornerstones of a Historic City* were designer Joyce Weston, editor Susanna Brougham, digital imaging wizard Al Mallette, mapmaker Mary Reilly, artist Jerry Butler, and indexer Dan Connolly. To them, to the authors and photographers, and to the many Salem residents who encouraged this project from its first glimmering, the publisher extends his heartfelt thanks.

—Webster Bull

Sunrise between Pickering Wharf and Shetland Properties, former site of the Naumkeag Mills. (Jim McAllister)

George Ropes, Jr., "Launching of the Ship Fame.*" (Peabody Essex Museum)*

The Maritime History of Salem

The saga of Salem begins on the sea with the arrival of the first permanent settlers to Cape Ann in 1623. In that year a small band of adventurers, with wives and families, constructed a fishing station near present-day Stage Fort Park in Gloucester. These hardy fisher-folk were sponsored by the Dorchester Company in England, which had invested thousands of pounds in the venture. The colonists had been sent to establish a profitable enterprise.

The leader of this tiny community of fewer than fifty souls was Master Roger Conant, a salter by trade from the town of Budleigh, Devonshire. When external conflicts and economic problems finally brought about the end of the Cape Ann station, it was Conant who led the determined remnant to a new home, which they called Naumkeag, in 1626.

Naumkeag, which means "the fishing place" in the language of local Native Americans, proved to be a far more satisfactory location for maritime activity. Here, Conant and his "Old Planters," as they came to be known, managed to reap a living from the sea. Back in England the Dorchester Company was selling out to the newly formed Massachusetts Bay Company in London. As a result, in 1628 a new governor, John Endecott, arrived aboard the *Abigail,* bringing more settlers and a

mandate to carve out of the wilderness a godly commonwealth. With Endecott the name of the place was changed from Naumkeag to Salem, the "place of peace." The name proved ironic in that Endecott was contentious and inflexible, alienating Roger Conant and the Old Planters and ultimately forcing them to cross the Bass River and settle in what would become the town of Beverly.

By the following summer, Salem's maritime industry expanded, with the establishment of Robert Moulton's boatyard along the South River Channel. He had brought with him apprentices to ensure that shipbuilding would flourish in Salem Harbor. Here small single-masted shallops were built to support the town's growing fishing activity.

With the arrival of newly appointed governor John Winthrop on the ship *Arbella* in June 1630, John Endecott was replaced and Salem ceased to be the Puritan capital in Massachusetts Bay. By August a rival port was founded at Boston. From this point on, these two maritime communities would challenge each other for dominance in fishing and commerce.

Salem turned to the sea in the 1630s, forced by the need to sustain a growing population that lacked sufficient food and fertile farmland. At this critical juncture Salem's fortunes took a turn for the better with the arrival of a new minister in 1636 to replace the exiled Roger Williams. The innovative Reverend Hugh Peter was deeply conscious of his spiritual responsibilities, yet recognized Salem's economic need for a fishing base. He recommended to the town that the common land at Winter Island, near the mouth of Salem Harbor, be set aside specifically for a fishing community.

In addition to the creation of a fishing station, Rev. Peter encouraged the building of a tavern on the island, the construction of a wharf and saltworks, and the laying out of Fish Street, which connected all the island's coastal facilities. He envisioned that codfish would become a principal export item, and to ensure Salem's ability to reach other coastal ports, he recommended that the town encourage the construction of larger vessels, such as two-masted ketches, capable of both fishing and trade.

The result of his efforts was spectacular. The offer of free land attracted many fishermen from other Massachusetts communities. Soon fish flakes (fish-drying stages) covered the coast, dozens of rude cottages rimmed the island, and fishing shallops were moored or drawn up on nearly every inch of shoreline. Salem's fishing fleet became a dominant commercial power, bringing in more than enough fish to meet the needs of its population.

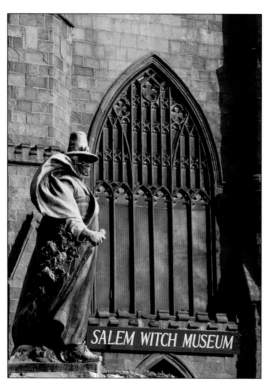

Statue of Roger Conant by Henry Kitson,
in front of the Salem Witch Museum.
(Jim McAllister)

West Indies trade

With a surplus of dried salt cod and a steady supply of lumber from the nearby virgin forests, Salem quickly established a profitable trade to other markets. In 1638, the trading vessel *Desire* arrived from the West Indies with a cargo of cotton, tobacco, and salt—for which the ship had exchanged Salem salt cod and lumber. Unfortunately, the return cargo also included a small shipment of West Indian slaves to be sold to local residents as domestic servants or field hands.

For the next century and a half Salem's economic foundation would be built upon this lucrative West Indies trade. Quickly it was discovered that the two most profitable West Indies products were sugar (either in loaf or cone form) and the ever-popular molasses. Molasses was doubly important to Salem's merchants, who could sell it as a sweetening agent or distill it into rum—a beverage of choice in both domestic and foreign markets. Consequently, many distilleries appeared in seventeenth-century Salem to provide merchants and sailors with prodigious quantities of New England rum-bullion. This product became yet another significant export.

By the 1660s Salem's maritime trade had developed

Winter Island, now the site of Salem Light, was set aside as a fishing community by Salem's first English settlers. Here, in 1799, shipbuilder Enos Briggs constructed, at public conscription, the frigate Essex—*at 850 tons and a cost of $95,000, the largest vessel ever built in Salem. The lighthouse was built in 1871. (Jim McAllister)*

The Turner House, or the House of the Seven Gables.
(Jim McAllister)

to such an extent that a merchant class began to form. They dominated the rich trade between the mainland and the "Sugar Islands," while extending their reach to include the maritime provinces of Canada, Bermuda, the Netherlands, the British Isles, and the "Wine Islands"— the Madeira Islands, the Azores, and the Canary Islands. From these far-flung sources Salem imported hides, fruit, wines, and pieces of eight—gold specie negotiable in any market. Salem's preeminent merchant of this era, Captain John Turner, arrived in port after a two-year absence in the Caribbean with so much gold that his neighbors whispered "piracy." By 1668, he had amassed enough of a fortune to purchase a choice piece of waterfront property for a new wharf, warehouse, and residence at the foot of what would become Turner Street. In later years, this oldest of Salem's merchant mansions would be immortalized by Nathaniel Hawthorne in *The House of the Seven Gables.* Among Turner's fleet, *Prosperous, John and Thomas,* and *Willing Mind* were the preeminent vessels that plied their trade from Turner's Wharf in Salem to the plantation owned by Turner's uncle in Barbados.

Also in the 1660s Great Britain issued the first so-called Navigation Acts, which gave American colonial vessels control of nearly all trade between the West Indies and the mainland. Thus Salem's trade grew and prospered, attracting more entrepreneurs such as the notable Philipe L'Anglois, who arrived from the Channel Islands during the 1660s and wisely anglicized his name to Philip English. He was only one of several prominent Salem merchants descended from French Huguenots

> "An hour's idleness is as bad as an hour's drunkenness."
> (Hugh Peter)

who emigrated to America for religious and commercial reasons. They continued to maintain trading links with the islands Guernsey and Jersey because, since the days of Henry VIII, neither island required the paying of customs duties, and thus greater profits were ensured.

Salem's diligent and hardworking Puritan seafarers believed that prosperity was an indication of divine favor, and they followed Hugh Peter's famous admonition that "an hour's idleness is as bad as an hour's drunkenness." Commercial setbacks were regarded as evidence of God's displeasure. For this reason, King Philip's War (1675) and King William's War (1689–97) were considered proof of God's unhappiness with the Puritan experiment in New England. Preachers warned that the young generation had lost sight of the original purpose of the Massachusetts Bay Colony and were preoccupied with the pursuit of "mammon."

In King Philip's War, the Native American population across New England destroyed dozens of frontier settlements, and in King William's War, French privateers devastated Salem's fishing and commercial fleet. (Privateers are private ships licensed by their government to attack and claim enemy ships.) In response to these depredations, Colonel John Turner—son of Captain John Turner—outfitted and commanded an armed cruiser, *Salem Galley,* which was sent by the town to attack French vessels in Canadian waters. It returned with several prizes (captured ships and their cargo) in 1693. Despite this success, French privateers reduced Salem's fleet from sixty vessels to only fifteen by the end of the year. Indeed, French privateers were free to attack and seize colonial vessels until the end of the war with France known as Queen Anne's War in 1713.

Nonetheless, the town continued to build ships and send them to sea. By 1699, twenty-six vessels were registered in Salem, two of which were rated at eighty tons or more. The remainder were sloops and ketches of twenty to forty tons. Miraculously, Salem struggled back to reestablish itself in foreign trade. But how exactly was this trade conducted? Consider the voyage of the Salem ship *Sarah,* which sailed for Barbados in September 1697 under the command of Captain Samuel Derby. She carried three hogsheads of fish for Colonel John Turner, one for Joseph Tyler, two for Philip English, two for John Browne (who also shipped a bay mare and two barrels of refuse fish), four hogsheads for Benjamin Browne, two hogsheads for Benjamin Pickman, three hogsheads of fish and four of mackerel for Habakkuk Gardner and five of haddock for William Hirst, as well as 5,550 red-oak barrel staves, "one bright sorrel horse with white face and four white feet," and 10,000 feet of white cedar shingles for Benjamin Allen, 6,900 red oak barrel staves for Benjamin Marston, and two hogsheads of scale fish and two boxes of candles for John Browne. (Any reference to fish in a Salem bill of lading refers only to cod.) This list gives the names of Salem's principal merchant shipowners at the dawn of the eighteenth century—all investing together in ventures and sharing the same risks and profits. Some owned vessels in partnership with others, some owned entire vessels, and others only freighted cargoes on vessels owned by their fellow merchants. The *Sarah* did not sell her cargo in Barbados as planned, but instead found a more desirable market in Antigua—another of Salem's primary destinations in the West Indies. The return cargo would usually consist of molasses, sugar, cotton, rum, and sometimes slaves.

Coastal trade also formed an important part of Salem's business activity at this time. Vessels loaded with lumber, salt fish, and rum made their way south, carefully rounding treacherous Cape Cod. They sometimes stopped at New York or Philadelphia and then continued on to Maryland and Virginia for tobacco and wheat and to South Carolina for rice and indigo. Salem's trade is remarkable not merely for the ingenious ways in which its merchants turned a profit, but also for the relative smallness of the vessels that carried Salem cargoes. An average pre-Revolutionary Salem vessel would carry one or two masts, would be about sixty to eighty feet on deck, and would displace less than one hundred tons burthen. Crews were as small as the vessel's size would allow—usually between four and six men, including officers.

Amazingly, these small vessels made regular voyages across the Atlantic, trading extensively with England, the Channel Islands, Spain, Portugal, the Azores, and the Madeira Islands. A vivid description of Salem's early eighteenth-century activities at sea is contained in a letter by British captain Nathaniel Uring, who visited the town in 1709:

> The inhabitants are very industrious and carry on a very considerable Trade to the Southern Plantations, viz. To all the Carribee Islands and Jamaica which they supply with Lumber as Plank, Boards, Joyce, and Shingles for building Houses, dried Fish and Salted Mackerel, some Beef, and Pork, Pitch, Tar; and Turpentine; Tallow and Bay Berry, Wax Candles; which last is made from wax that is extracted from a

Designed to resemble a ship's cabin, the headquarters of the Salem Marine Society, founded in 1766, is now located on the roof of the Hawthorne Hotel. (Jim McAllister)

berry that grows in plenty in that country. They send also several ships to the Bay of Honduras to load Logwood, and have some trade to Carolina, Virginia and Maryland, Pennsylvania and New York; they likewise send many ships to Portugal and the Straights with dry'd codfish which is generally called "Poor Jack," or Baccalew; and have a very good trade to the Isles of Azores and Madeira, whom they furnish with pipe staves, dry'd fish, Salted Mackeral and Bees-Wax; for which they purchase wines and return to New England. All the country of New England takes off great quantities of the British Manufactures and in return, build us ships and send us whale oyl and bone, great quantities of Turpentine, Pitch and Tar, some furs and deerskins; besides which many ships from England lade with dry'd fish for the Straights and Portugal.

Pirates

These Salem vessels not only faced natural disasters—storms, epidemics and such—but were often subject to the depredations of pirates as well. Consider the harrowing tale of Salem's Captain Shattock, who in 1719, while making his way to Salem from the West Indies aboard the brig *Endeavor,* faced this encounter:

Within sight of ye Bohemia Islands [the Bahamas] known by ye name of Long Island at 3 of ye clock [in the] afternoon we unhapily met with a Pyrat being a Brigg of 12 Gunns & one hundred and twenty men, one Capt. Charles Vain Commander, who took me & kept me about four Days—carried me to an Island called Crooked Island [and] plundered and rifled me of Severall [hogsheads] of rum, a parcel of British

Merchandise, five barrels of powder, 30 sides of leather, 84 pewter dishes, and ye most of our provisions. [The pirates] stript the Brigg of what suted them, took away my clearing certificates and other papers of value. [They] stript my people of their cloathes & abused some of them.

Piracy occasionally took place in Salem Harbor itself. As the Salem sloop *Squirrel* was about to enter the port under the command of Captain Andrew Haraden, she was taken by the notorious pirate Captain John Philip. Transferring his pirate crew to the *Squirrel* and taking Haraden as a hostage, Captain Philip set the merchant crew adrift. In ten days' time, the plucky Haraden had persuaded the pirates to mutiny, killing Philip and some of his loyal followers. The *Squirrel* sailed back to Cape Ann with Philip's head hanging at the masthead as a warning to other plunderers of Salem's peaceful trade. Incidentally, Haraden's grandson Jonathan proved to be Salem's preeminent privateer captain during the American Revolution.

For Salem, the events leading to the outbreak of that struggle began during the 1760s, when England's Parliament attempted to raise revenue by applying taxes to certain imported commodities. The British wanted to tighten their control of American trading practices and to force American merchants and their sailing captains to pay appropriate customs taxes. Salem's shipowning merchants were as guilty as any in the colonies in attempting to circumnavigate the various acts of trade, and for nearly one hundred years they engaged in illicit practices, including smuggling. As a result of this change in British policy, the following notice was issued by the

> Piracy occasionally took place in Salem Harbor itself.

frustrated collector of customs concerning what Salem's shipowning merchants could expect in the future:

Custom House
Port of Salem
December 26, 1763

Whereas it has been repre-sented to the Right Honourable the Lords Commissioners of His Majesty's Treasury, that many vessels trading to the Plantations not belonging to the King of Great Britain, and returning with cargoes of rum, sugar and molasses, have found the means to smuggle the same into his Majesty's colonies, without paying the King's Duty. This is to inform all Masters of said Vessels using the Said Trade, that they are hereby strictly required on their arrival here, to enter or report their Ships and Cargoes at the Custom House, when proper Officers will be put on board such Vessels, to see that the Act of the Sixth of his late Majesty King George the Second (imposing a duty on all Foreign Rum, Sugar and Molasses) be in all its parts fully carried into Execution. By Order of the Surveyor-General,

J. Cockle, Collector
J. Dowse, Surveyor & Searcher

The Derby homestead, 27 Herbert Street, where Salem's greatest sea trader, Elias Haskett Derby, grew up.
(Jim McAllister)

Certain Salem shipowners were carrying on trade without regard to British maritime law, especially during the French and Indian War (1756–1763). During this conflict, young, enterprising Salem captains took advantage of the increased demand for goods to supply not only the British, but also the French. One of the most celebrated cases of this divided loyalty involved Captain Richard Derby, who had only recently left his job as a sea captain sailing for the old merchant House of Orne in order to begin his own merchant business. ("House of" referred to a business enterprise dominated by one family.) It seems that in 1759, at the height of the struggle between France and England, Derby's schooner *Three Brothers* was seized three days out of the French port of St. Eustatia by the British privateer *King of Prussia*. The Derby vessel was under the command of Salem captain Michael Driver and was carrying a cargo of fish, wine, oil, and raisins, as well as 797 pieces of eight. She was declared a prize and her cargo confiscated, since she was trading with the enemy during wartime. Derby was infuriated and submitted a claim to the British government for the loss of his cargo and ship in the amount of 1,334 pounds, yet received nothing for his trouble. Not surprisingly, when the

Revolution finally did erupt, Captain Richard Derby, Sr., and his three sons, Elias Haskett, John, and Richard, Jr., would be in the forefront of the patriotic privateering effort out of Salem.

By the 1760s, Salem had become a major seaport in almost every respect. Its residents numbered only about forty-five hundred, and the level of business activity was remarkable for that population size. Winter Island still served as the primary fishing base, although fish flakes dotted the whole coastline—especially on Stage Point, where the present-day Shetland Properties facility stands. Ship construction had also become a major shoreline activity. Shipyards had originally been limited primarily to the "inner harbor" area near present-day Riley Plaza near the mouth of Ruck's Creek—a place known in those days as "Knocker's Hole"—behind the present U.S. Post Office. By the 1760s however, most shipbuilding businesses had moved to the outer harbor. The most prominent of these was the Becket Shipyard, operated by the Becket Family and located at the foot of Becket Street, near the present-day New England Power Plant. Rope and cordage, so essential to ship construction, were conveniently produced at local ropewalks operated by the Vincent and Sparhawk families and located to the east of the Common—ultimately extending into Collins Cove. Sails were made in lofts situated in the upper levels of the stores and warehouses lining the northern waterfront of the South River, whose more than twenty busy wharves bustled with activity.

The largest and busiest of Salem's wharves in the pre-Revolutionary era was Union Wharf, which joined Jeggle's Island to the shore of the South River by means of a drawbridge. It had been constructed in the 1720s as a collective venture by a group of merchants who named

it Union as a token of their cooperative spirit. Today it is known as Pickering Wharf, and it entirely occupies the drawbridge and island areas, which are buried deep below its surface. From this wharf the famous Derby and Crowninshield merchant families began their shipping activities in the 1750s.

Captain Richard Derby built his house across from the wharf at the corner of Herbert Street and Derby Street, near his place of business. Here too, in 1761, he acquired additional property closer to the mouth of the South River and began construction of Derby Wharf. This facility would serve as the primary base for Derby privateers during the Revolution and would be extended to a length of almost a half mile by the turn of the nineteenth century.

By the 1760s Richard Derby, Sr., had retired from the sea, but he was still active in shipping activities. Having learned his trade from the great Salem merchant Timothy Orne, Derby understood the importance of increasing and diversifying his holdings to minimize the possibility of disaster resulting from a single business reversal. This shrewdness in judgment made him a leader in Salem's maritime industry. At a time when most merchants had partial interest in only one or two vessels, by 1765 the House of Derby controlled eight vessels—all engaged in foreign trade. Derby schooled his sons in the secrets of making a profit; of them, Elias Haskett Derby would become the greatest merchant in Salem's history. But the heyday of the Derbys would arrive after the Revolution. For now, the town's most prosperous merchant was Colonel Benjamin Pickman, who was engaged in both fishing and commercial trade. Commercial rivals, Pickman and Derby were also on opposite sides of the fence politically, the former would remain a British

Pickering Wharf, originally Union Wharf. (Jim McAllister)

Site of the London Coffee House on Central Street, meeting place of the Salem Chapter of the Sons of Liberty prior to and during the Revolution. (Jim McAllister)

loyalist, while the latter would lead the town's Revolutionary faction.

Patriots and loyalists

The American Revolution was the great turning point for Salem's maritime history. The social and commercial establishments of pre-Revolution times would be forever changed. The old merchant families, such as the Turners, the Brownes, the Ornes, and the Pickmans, had risen in the seventeenth and early eighteenth centuries and tended to remain loyal to the Crown. They had lost their position of leadership by the 1770s. In contrast, the newly established merchants such as the Derbys, the Cabots, and the Crowninshields saw the coming conflict as an opportunity to replace the old Puritan "codfish aristocracy" with a "natural aristocracy" of talented, self-taught entrepreneurs who had succeeded in "pulling themselves up by their own bootstraps." Consequently, in the years prior to the outbreak of hostilities, Salem was split between the majority patriotic faction and the minority loyalist element. The town soon became the scene of serious Revolutionary activities and protests.

Salem's troubles began in 1761 with the appointment of James Cockle as surveyor of the port. Since it was his duty to strictly enforce British trade regulations, which, although on the books for years, had never been closely followed, he began by seizing vessels and their cargoes for nonpayment of customs duty. This policy quickly incurred the wrath of many of Salem's merchants and captains, as well as the people who worked for them. They questioned whether the British govern-

> The American Revolution was the great turning point for Salem's maritime history.

ment, which was not elected by American subjects, legally had the right to impose laws for which no American had voted or given consent. Those hundreds of people whose livelihoods depended upon the success and profitability of Salem's trade took issue with Cockle and the government he represented. When the Stamp Act was put into effect in 1765, Salem, like many other towns, voted unanimously to "put an entire stop to their Trade rather than make use of any Stamped Papers."

Salem's citizenry sought to protect the economic interests and freedoms of the community by physically stopping the efforts of Salem's customs officials. On September 7, 1768, an alleged spy for the Custom House was charged with being an informer. The unfortunate Robert Wood was seized by the mob, stripped of his clothing, set upon a hogshead barrel, tarred and feathered, and then carried through the streets of the town. Several days later, Thomas Rowe, a Custom House worker, unwisely informed a customs officer that a Salem vessel was seeking to evade customs duty. The worker too was seized and dragged from the waterfront to the Common to be tarred and feathered. He rode through the streets of Salem with signs upon his chest and back bearing the single word INFORMER. From 1768 onward, Salem's waterfront was ruled by the patriotic mob.

By 1770, this more radical element was led by a newly arrived Presbyterian, the Reverend Nathaniel Whitaker. Whitaker's anti-British sermons further inflamed the dock workers, mechanics, sailors, and laborers who comprised his sizable congregation at the Tabernacle Church. Until the outbreak of the war, viru-

"Beverly Privateer and her Prize." (Beverly Historical Society)

lent anti-Tory feeling swept through the town, manifested in numerous incidents of lawlessness and violence. Shortly after the Boston Massacre, public pressure was brought to bear upon those few merchants who violated the anti-importation agreement and sold British goods in Salem. They were forced by the town to remove their stock and place it in warehouses. The windows of Anglican St. Peter's Church were smashed, and loyalist judge Nathaniel Ropes, dying from smallpox, was forced to plead with the mob to stop attacking his home on Essex Street.

When the Boston Sons-of-Liberty dumped 342 chests of tea into Boston Harbor in 1773, Boston was punished with the Boston Port Act, closing the port. Because the colonial government could not operate out of a closed port, the newly appointed governor, Thomas Gage, moved the colonial capital to Salem in 1774. Consequently, on June 1, 1774, the Massachusetts House of Representatives met in the Old Court House building located near the middle of present-day Washington Street.

Salem's patriotic merchants, wishing to sympathize with the plight of their Boston colleagues, published the following statement:

> We are deeply affected with the sense of our public calamities: But the miseries that are now rapidly hastening on our brethren in the capital of the province greatly excite our commiseration. By shutting up the port of Boston some imagine that the course of trade might be turned hither, and to our benefit; but Nature in the formation of our harbour, forbids our becoming rivals in commerce to that convenient mart. And were it otherwise,—we must be dead to every idea of justice—lost to all the feelings of humanity could we indulge one thought to seize on wealth, and raise our fortunes on the ruin of our suffering neighbors.

Nevertheless, Salem did benefit by receiving vessels that otherwise would have gone to the port of Boston. But a great deal more than ship cargoes were being stored at Salem in 1774. It had become one of the primary repositories for militia weapons and munitions in Essex County.

The Salem militia unit, known as the First Essex Regiment, had already rid itself of its loyalist colonel, William Browne, and in turn elected Colonel Timothy Pickering as commander. Colonel Pickering quickly began to organize patriotic military resistance at Salem by stockpiling war matériel, a fact that was soon conveyed to Governor-General Gage, who, on Sunday, February 26, 1775, dispatched by ship the Sixty-fourth Regiment of Foot under the command of Colonel Leslie, from Castle William in Boston Harbor to Marblehead. Leslie landed in Marblehead and proceeded to march his troops toward Salem.

The news of Leslie's advance was brought to Salem on horseback by Marblehead's Major John Pedrick, who made the announcement at the Second Congregational Church of Rev. Thomas Barnard, who was then holding services. Immediately, the Salem militia sprang into action and dispatched a unit to secure the guns and munitions in storage in North Salem. Riders were sent to

> The first blood of the Revolution was spilled in Salem over a month before the outbreak of hostilities at Lexington and Concord.

other North Shore communities, whose companies of minutemen were soon on the march to Salem. By the time of Leslie's arrival, the North Bridge, which was a drawbridge, was drawn up, preventing the British from crossing to North Salem to conduct their inspection. The entire town was in a state of hostile readiness, and lined up along the north bank of the North River was the Salem militia regiment, prepared for a military confrontation.

Several flatboats were lying on the bank near Leslie's troops. To prevent their use by the soldiers, three Salem men went to chop holes in the hulls. Leslie ordered his troops to stop them, and one Salemite, Joseph Whicher, dared the soldiers to stab him with their bayonets. One veteran obliged, and thus the first blood of the Revolution was spilled in Salem over a month before the outbreak of hostilities at Lexington and Concord.

The episode could have resulted in many deaths but for the intervention of Rev. Barnard, who served as negotiator. Colonel Leslie was aware that he clearly had lost the element of surprise. He also knew that hundreds of militiamen from all over Essex County were on the march to Salem. Seeking to fulfill only the letter of his orders, he suggested that if he were allowed to cross the bridge, he would march his troops no more than fifty

Mansion house of Elias Haskett Derby designed by Charles Bulfinch and Samuel McIntire and finished in 1799. (Beverly Historical Society)

yards, turn around, and return to his vessel in Marblehead. It was agreed, and further bloodshed was averted.

With anti-British sentiments running high, it is not surprising that when the Revolution did break out, the Salem Bay ports of Salem, Beverly, and Marblehead would lead the thirteen colonies in the number and success of privateering efforts against England. Their major contribution in the war at sea began shortly after the battles of Lexington and Concord and ended only slightly after the signing of the Treaty of Paris in 1783.

During the siege of Boston, which lasted from the summer of 1775 to March 1776, Salem's neighboring port of Beverly served as General George Washington's naval base. From here armed Continental cruisers, commissioned as vessels-of-war under the command of Washington, sailed in search of English transports and merchant ships. Their purpose was to cut off supplies to the British-held city. Of these, the *Hannah*, a topsail schooner owned by Colonel John Glover of Marblehead, was the first. In September 1775, she sailed under the command of Captain Nicholas Broughton and captured the ship *Unity*, which was loaded with lumber and supplies for Boston's garrison.

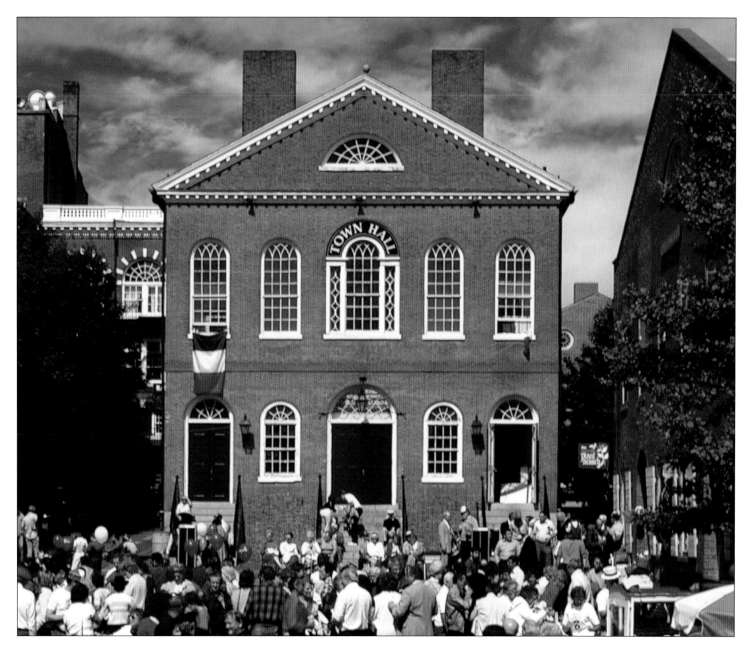

Old Town Hall in Derby Square, opened in 1816 on the site of the Derby mansion, shown opposite. (Jim McAllister)

One of the most exciting local episodes of the Revolution involved the *Hannah*. As she attempted to leave Salem Harbor, she was sighted by the British sloop of war H.M.S. *Nautilus*, which immediately gave chase. Not wishing to take on the heavily armed warship, the *Hannah* reversed course and returned to Beverly Harbor, with the *Nautilus* in hot pursuit. Fortunately, the tide was ebbing, and the shallow-drafted *Hannah* managed to outrun her adversary, skimming over a sandbar that a few minutes later caught the *Nautilus*. The resulting exchange of cannon fire concluded with several shots aimed at Beverly's meetinghouse. Then the *Nautilus* lay on her side, entirely stranded in the middle of the harbor.

Meanwhile, both the Salem and Beverly militia brought their fieldpieces to the shoreline and placed the hapless *Nautilus* in a crossfire from both the Salem and Beverly sides. The confrontation ended with the death of one British sailor and no American casualties. The *Nautilus* righted herself at high tide and sailed from the harbor, never to return.

Privateers

Shortly after this event, in November 1775, Salem's first independent privateer, the schooner *Dolphin,* captured the British sloop *Success*. This was only the beginning of Salem's career as a privateering port. During the course of the war, Salem and Beverly—which was included in the Salem Custom House district—sent out over 332 privateers, over 10 percent of the total number sent out by all thirteen colonies together!

A popular ballad, entitled "Bold Daniel," was composed in the honor of Nathaniel Hawthorne's grandfather, the captain of a Salem privateer.

To take to the sea as a privateer, an American merchant was required to post a bond equivalent to between $5,000 and $10,000 to insure that the captain, officers, and crew would carefully follow the privateering articles and never attempt to capture a vessel of neutral or allied countries. Merchants and some private citizens would then purchase shares from the prospective privateer, putting up capital to provide the ship with cannon, supplies, and munitions. A captain would be contracted for a large share of the proceeds. He had to be a man of considerable ability. He was required not only to command a crew, but also to capture vessels on the high seas—by force. Oversized crews were then hired—each man serving for a share of the money gained from the sale of prizes (ships and cargo) taken during the voyage. If lucky, these sailors could return to discover themselves financially well off. Or they might find out that their prizes had been recaptured and none sailed back to be sold at auction. In such cases, all participants in the venture had wasted their time and money. Privateering was a highly speculative venture, but captains such as Salem's Jonathan Haraden and Beverly's Hugh Hill were especially talented in this particular calling and earned huge profits for the merchants.

In 1776 the Salem privateering industry got fully underway. In June, Elias Haskett Derby's schooner *Sturdy Beggar* made three cruises and initiated the Derbys into a new and very profitable wartime industry. They did especially well at privateering. Later, in just one year, the Derby-owned brigantine *Fame,* carrying sixteen

The Friendship, *which served as both trader and privateer for the Salem firm of Peirce & Waitt. Today a replica is on view at Central Wharf.*
(Peabody Essex Museum)

A Guided Tour of Salem's Maritime Past

1. Pioneer Village Simple wooden shelters like those built by Salem's first English settlers are on view at this recreation in Forest River Park, completed in 1930 and restored during the 1980s.

2. Winter Island Early settlers used this land near the mouth of Salem Harbor as a fishing base. There was a fort here during the Revolution, and in 1799 it was the site of the construction of the frigate *Essex,* largest vessel ever built in Salem. The lighthouse was built in 1871.

3. Turner House The oldest of Salem's merchant mansions was built in 1668 for Captain John Turner. Originally the property included a warehouse and wharf. Today it is better known as the House of the Seven Gables.

4. Peabody Essex Museum Founded in 1799 as the East India Marine Society, the Peabody Museum, as it became known, merged in 1992 with the Essex Institute. Today, the museum is the most important repository of artifacts and documents related to Salem's maritime past.

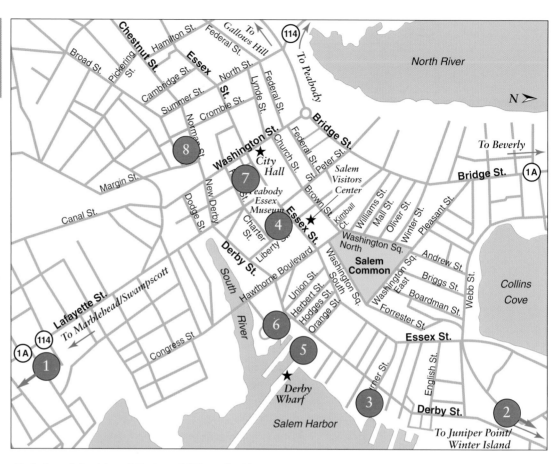

5. Salem Maritime National Historic Site Created in 1938 and maintained today by the U.S. Park Service, the site includes Central Wharf with a typical warehouse, Derby Wharf, the Custom House where Nathaniel Hawthorne worked, Hawkes House, Derby House, Narbonne House, the West India Goods Store, and a replica of the merchant vessel *Friendship.*

6. Pickering Wharf Originally Union Wharf, the largest of the pre-Revolutionary wharves, and now an important waterfront development.

7. Old Town Hall (site of Derby Mansion) The grandest mansion of Salem's greatest merchant, Elias Hasket Derby, stood on this site for just seventeen years, from 1799 to 1816.

8. Site of Knocker's Hole Today the U.S. Post Office Building, like much of downtown Salem, sits on fill covering what was once a bustling waterfront. Knocker's Hole was the site of early shipyards.

guns and one hundred men would send back to Salem a ship, three brigantines, a schooner, and two sloops. These would be declared legal prizes and subsequently auctioned off together with their cargoes. Among *Sturdy Beggar*'s several masters was Captain Daniel Hathorne, the grandfather of Nathaniel Hawthorne. Hathorne was so successful in the early years of the war that a popular ballad, entitled "Bold Daniel," was composed in his honor.

Another privateer, who would later became one of Salem's great merchants, was Captain Simon Forrester. In 1776, he took command of the heavily armed sloop *Rover,* owned by merchants Jacob Ashton and Joseph Sprague. Under Forrester's command Rover distinguished herself in capturing the brigantines *Mary and James, Diana, Good Intent,* and *Mary Ann* as well as the sloop *James* before the end of the year. Captain Forrester was originally from Ireland and had been brought to America by Captain Hathorne. He grew up in the Hathorne household on Union Street and ultimately married the daughter of "bold Daniel." He was renowned for his skill as both a captain and later a successful merchant. He was equally famous for his capacity for drink and his violent temper.

Many of the names of Salem's privateering vessels vividly indicate the patriotic excitement and aggressive feelings that influenced the maritime activities of the town until the conclusion of hostilities in 1783. The House of Cabot sent out *Terrible Creature* and *Oliver Cromwell. The Terrible Creature,* in 1778, tweaked the pride of the British navy by capturing the sloop *Susannah,* which was loaded with provisions for British general Richard Howe in Philadelphia. Derby's *Scorpion* was assigned to the West Indies—a popular hunting ground for Salem privateers—where it narrowly escaped capture by the British navy on several occasions. Avoiding the British navy was essential to success as a privateer, since no privately armed vessel was equal to the task of taking on a ship-of-the-line. Capture doomed Salem privateers to imprisonment in Halifax or England—often on board damp, unheated hulks moored in an isolated part of some harbor. Since American privateering commissions were not recognized as legitimate by the British government, captured American seamen thought themselves fortunate not to be hanged as pirates.

Not all encounters with heavily armed ships resulted in a defeat, however. One of the most famous of Salem's Revolutionary privateers was the *Franklin,* a brigantine of two hundred tons owned jointly by the Cabots of Beverly and Bartholomew Putnam. She carried eighteen guns. A few days after leaving Salem, she was challenged by the powerful British privateer ship *Enterprise,* of Bristol. After a hotly contested battle, the *Franklin* succeeded in capturing the larger Britisher, which was ordered to Salem with a prize crew. Sadly, the *Enterprise* was soon recaptured by the H.M.S. *Amphytrite* and was sent to Halifax.

Indeed, throughout the Revolution, Salem was constantly guarded by a British blockade seeking to intercept and capture all American vessels entering or leaving the port. Conversely, the harbor was protected throughout the war by forts on Juniper Point and Winter Island, as well as by batteries located at Beverly and Marblehead. The Winter Island fort had been present since the seventeenth century and had changed its name several times with the fortunes of war and the shifting of royal houses. From 1776 onward it would be named

Fort Pickering, for Salem's Revolutionary militia commander who would later serve on General Washington's staff. Surmounting both the Juniper Point Battery and Fort Pickering was a new Revolutionary fort, Fort Lee.

Privateering helped supply the home front and the armies in the field with goods that could not otherwise be manufactured or imported. It also provided a livelihood to hundreds of unemployed seamen and maritime craftspeople. Most importantly, privateering forced the British navy to assign dozens of vessels to patrol the shipping lanes from the maritime provinces in Canada to the West Indies and even to the English Channel and the Irish Sea, keeping them from active duty. It also drove British maritime insurance rates sky-high. This caused British mercantile interests to pressure Parliament to bring the war to a speedy conclusion.

By 1781, many Salem vessels were sailing not only with privateering commissions, but also with "letters of marque and reprisal," which allowed them to conduct trade on the high seas; if the occasion arose, they were permitted to attack and capture a prize. Beverly captain Hugh Hill, sailing the letter-of-marque ship *Cicero,* en route to Cadiz, decided to do some privateering and captured the ship *Mercury.* It was carrying, along with cargo, over 15,000 pounds in gold. Perhaps more important than gold was the plunder taken by Captain Jonathan Haraden, who was credited with capturing from British vessels over one thousand cannons that served the American cause.

At war's end, the Derbys and the Cabots were by far the richer for their efforts and fared better than any other local merchants (some actually lost more vessels than they captured). Fittingly, the last great privateering prize was taken by the Derby ship *Grand Turk,* stationed off St. Kitts in the West Indies on March 12, 1783. Her captain, Thomas Pratt, sighted the four-hundred-ton merchantman *Pompey,* en route from London. The British captain welcomed Pratt with the news that the Treaty of Paris had just been signed, that the Revolution was over, and that peace now existed between the United States and England. The skeptical Captain Pratt took the ship anyway and brought her back to Salem, where she was declared a prize by the court. Ironically, this Derby prize was bought at auction by Derby's great rival, George Crowninshield, and was renamed the *America.*

> "Those who five years ago were the meaner people, are now, by a strange revolution become almost the only men of power, riches and influence."
> (Samuel Curwen)

Salem's Golden Age

When Cornwallis surrendered to Washington at Yorktown, the military musicians played "The World Turned Upside Down." The same can be said for the world of maritime Salem. The exiled loyalist Samuel Curwen tersely wrote the following about his hometown at the end of the Revolution: "Those who five years ago were the meaner people, are now, by a strange revolution become almost the only men of power, riches and influence. The Cabots of Beverly, who, you know, had but five years ago a very moderate share of property, are now said to be by far the most wealthy in New England; Haskett Derby claims the second place in that list."

These two great merchants, John Cabot and Elias Haskett Derby, pulled Salem out of its brief postwar depression and launched Salem's "Golden Age." In 1783, Cabot was already testing new European markets. In that year, his ship *Buccannier* touched at several Baltic ports and finally reached the Russian port of St. Petersburg. His was the first American vessel to trade there. Following almost immediately in his wake, Elias Haskett Derby sent his ship *Light Horse* in 1784 and reached St. Petersburg in August with a cargo of sugar. These voyages marked the beginning of the lucrative Russian trade whereby American and West Indian produce was exchanged for iron, furs, and hemp sailcloth known as "Russian duck."

Five months after the *Light Horse* had sailed for the Baltic, Derby sent his *Grand Turk* to the Cape of Good Hope under the command of Captain Jonathan Ingersoll. Ingersoll hoped to convince returning British East India captains to "break bulk" and sell Chinese tea at Cape Town prior to their return voyage to England. While there he conversed with the master of the New York ship *Empress of China*, the first American vessel to visit Canton. Ingersoll convinced the captain of the British East Indiaman *Calcutta* to sell his cargo of two hundred chests of Hyson tea in exchange for good New England rum, which Ingersoll promised to deliver to the British

At the peak of Salem's Golden Age, wharfside warehouses groaned with exotic goods. (Mark Sexton)

garrison at St. Helena in the South Atlantic. Even more fortunate for Derby was the information that Ingersoll delivered, stating that American ships could reach and be admitted to trade at Canton.

On December 3, 1785, the *Grand Turk* sailed again, the first Salem vessel to clear for any port east of the Cape of Good Hope. She was under the command of Captain Ebenezer West with Mr. William Vans as supercargo. She carried a cargo of tobacco, pitch, tar, rice, flour, butter, wine, iron, sugar, fish, oil, chocolate, prunes, ginseng, beef, brandy, rum, bacon, hams, cheese, candles, earthenware, and beer, for a value of 7,183 pounds, 5 shillings, and 4 pence. By September 1786, she had reached Canton and begun the elaborate negotiations that were standard business practice between China and Western businessmen until the mid–nineteenth century. This began Salem's China Trade, one of its most profitable maritime connections.

The *Grand Turk* returned safely to Salem on the morning of May 22, 1787, with a full press of sail as she rounded Naugus Head and fired the customary salute to announce her arrival. She was the first New England vessel to return from China, and the curiosity of Salem's inhabitants knew no bounds. The vessel was swamped in a harbor filled with skiffs and various craft filled with people curious to discover what exotic merchandise she had brought back from the mysterious East.

This first voyage was in many respects representative of hundreds of later ones, and the vessel returned with a typical assortment of Chinese goods— Bohea, Hyson, Souchong, Cassia, and Canzo teas, boxes, ox hides, chamois skins (anglicized to "shammy"), muslin, and paper. Missing from this shipment, but common to later ones, were silk textiles. The *Grand Turk* on this voyage made over "twice more capital than she carried out," and the China trade in general earned very high profits. E. H. Derby led Salem in opening and developing this market, but not content with one destination in the East, he sought more.

By 1787, Derby had decided to establish a base for his Far Eastern operations at Isle de France (modern-day Mauritius). To that end he sent his son, Elias H. Derby, Jr., then about twenty years of age, in command of the *Grand Turk*. Derby intended to settle his son at Isle de France to serve as company agent. As was his custom, E. H. Derby, Sr., gave his son instructions to sell the ship if it was financially advantageous—an opportunity that arose when a French merchant offered $13,000 for the *Grand Turk*. Since this was nearly twice the amount of the vessel's assessed value, the famous Salem merchantman was sold into French service.

At home in Salem, Derby's fleet continued to grow, and he continued to send vessels to his new base of operations at Isle de France. Each voyage earned the House

> The most lucrative of all Salem's maritime trades was the Sumatran pepper trade.

of Derby amazing profits. In the meantime, E. H. Derby, Jr., began to purchase vessels as well and initiated a brisk and profitable freighting business with nearby India. He began in 1788 by trading for cotton goods with the port of Bombay. His vessels, the *Peggy* and the *Sultana*, were the first American ships to visit that port. Soon E. H. Derby, Jr., controlled American trade with the ports of Bombay, Madras, and Calcutta.

Derby activity in the Far East at this time was tremendous. For example, in February 1789, E. H. Derby, Sr., sent his ship *Astrea* to the Dutch colony of Batavia in the East Indies. She arrived at Java Head on July 13, 1789, to discover the Derby ship *Three Sisters* already there. Batavia was an excellent source at this time for tin, sugar, spices, bird's nests (made into bird's nest soup—a delicacy in China), sandalwood, beeswax, coffee, and, most valuable of all, pepper. Soon, the *Astrea* and the *Three Sisters* reached the port of Canton and were still loading cargo when two more Derby vessels, the *Atlantic* and the *Light Horse*, also arrived. They had been sent from Isle de France by E. H. Derby, Jr.

Since a total of fifteen American ships had traded in Canton that season, the prices of American goods had dropped, and the increased demand for tea had caused its price to rise. Consequently, in order to ensure a profit on the venture, the Derby agents decided to sell two vessels, invest the proceeds in more Chinese tea, and ship all the crew and cargoes home to Salem in the remaining two vessels. Accordingly, the *Atlantic* was sold for $6,600 and the *Three Sisters* for $4,000. The proceeds

Looking out the harbor from Crowninshield Wharf, in a detail from the painting by George Ropes, Jr. (Peabody Essex Museum)

were invested in 728,871 pounds of tea. This cargo was then loaded onto the *Astrea* and the *Light Horse,* which sailed from Canton on January 22, 1790.

The *Astrea* arrived in Salem on June 1, 1790, and the *Light Horse* on June 15. The night of her arrival witnessed a fierce storm, causing her to drag her anchor and come within yards of the rocks of Marblehead Harbor. Fortunately for Derby, both vessels landed safely at Derby Wharf and off-loaded the largest cargo of tea up to that time.

Together the *Astrea* and *Light Horse* were assessed $25,000 in duties by the newly established U.S. Custom Service. This represented a huge unexpected expense that would also flood the market with tea and drive the price downward. To avoid having to pay all the tax at

once, Derby petitioned Congress to allow him to store his cargo temporarily in a bonded warehouse and pay his customs taxes as he was able to sell quantities over time. Congress granted his request and in so doing established the U.S. Custom Service's bonded warehouse system.

The most lucrative of all Salem's maritime trades was the Sumatran pepper trade, which it controlled for a number of years. How Salem merchants discovered the source of pepper still remains a mystery. Certainly the credit is due to Captain Jonathan Carnes who, either on an exploratory voyage in the brig *Cadet* in 1788 or else on the Derby ship *Grand Sachem* in 1793, found that wild pepper was harvested on the northwest coast of Sumatra. In any case, Carnes did not share his know-

The Custom House, Hawkes House, and Derby House stand side by side at the heart of Salem's waterfront. (Mark Sexton)

ledge with anyone but members of his family—his uncles Willard and Jonathan Peele. These merchants built the 120-ton schooner *Rajah* in 1795, made Carnes the master, and promptly sent him and the *Rajah* "for India." The Rajah vanished into the Indian Ocean and was not heard from for eighteen months until she returned in July 1797, heavily laden with a bulk cargo of pepper that earned her owners a 700 percent profit.

This was only the beginning. Over the next five years, Carnes made several voyages in the *Rajah* to Sumatra, bringing back over 400,000 pounds of pepper before other Salem merchants discovered where the source lay. Soon Derby's great competitors, the Crowninshields would be trading extensively for pepper and sending their flagship, *America,* and the *Belisarius* to join with the *Rajah* in the search for pepper. Other great Salem merchant ships, George Peabody's *Cincinnatus* and Stephen Phillips's *Union,* imported millions of pounds—far more than could be consumed at home. Much of it was reexported to the markets of Europe, breaking the power of the Dutch East India Company, which for years had dominated the flow of pepper to the Continent. Salem continued in this profitable trade longer than in most others—ending it only in 1846.

End of an era

The apogee and sudden decline of Salem's career as a seaport came with the turn of the nineteenth century, as the infamous "Jefferson Embargo" brought the Golden Age to an abrupt end. By this time, Elias Haskett Derby had passed from the scene. He and his wife had both died in their great mansion in 1799. The power of the Federalists was on the wane, and the Jeffersonian Republicans were now led by the Crowninshields in Salem.

The world was once again locked in an international struggle, this time between Napoleon's France and Great Britain. President Thomas Jefferson kept the United States neutral by preventing American vessels from trading with both France and Great Britain, as well as with their respective allies. The embargo required that no American vessel clear an American port to engage in international commerce. This policy aimed at denying American goods to both belligerents and forcing them to stop illegal seizures of neutral American shipping and the impressment of American seamen. It did not achieve its objectives. It did, however, bring Salem's shipping to a standstill from December 1807 until March 1809. During that time over one hundred Salem ships lay idle. Ship construction virtually ceased, and thousands of maritime craftspeople, dockworkers, sailors, and all their families lacked incomes.

The Federalist merchants railed against this disastrous policy. Only the Crowninshields and William Gray, among the most wealthy of the town, upheld the wisdom of the embargo as a deterrent to war. With the repeal of the embargo, William Gray and his family, once staunch Federalists, were ostracized for their anti-Federalist sentiments. Gray moved his home, business operations, and ships—which amounted to about one third of the registered tonnage of Salem—to Boston in 1809.

Salem never completely recovered from the terrible

> The infamous "Jefferson Embargo" brought the Golden Age to an abrupt end.

effects of the embargo. Six days after its repeal, six vessels cleared for Sumatra, Europe, and the West Indies. By the end of March 1809, twenty-two more vessels had left Salem for Canton, Sumatra, and the Baltic Sea. Yet irrevocable damage had been done. Lost income and lack of capital from shipping crippled the development of domestic enterprises. Canals, highways, mills, house construction, bridges, aqueducts, and numerous other public and private projects could not be undertaken without the profits of foreign trade to underwrite them. To make matters worse, the War of 1812 forced Salem to curtail trade again. Once more the city's merchants resorted to wartime privateering.

Not surprisingly, the Republican faction took to privateering against England with almost Revolutionary zeal. The Crowninshield family, led by George Crowninshield and Benjamin W. Crowninshield, were the first to launch privateers—a mere four days after war with England was declared. The first was the *Jefferson*, followed quickly by the *Fame*. Within ten more days sailed *Polly* and the schooners *Dolphin, Buckskin, Regulator, Fair Trader,* and *Active*. Most famous of all was the Crowninshield ship *America*, which in 1812 began her career by capturing six prizes sold at auction in Salem for a total of $158,000. During her second cruise, under the command of Captain John Kehew, she took ten more prizes and narrowly escaped capture by the British warship *La Hogue*.

During the course of the war, Salem sent out at least forty privateers. Unfortunately, only about thirteen

> Hawthorne mourned the slow death of the port and hearkened back to the days of "King Derby."

escaped capture or destruction. Much of Salem's merchant fleet remained at home, and most that ventured forth to trade were captured. By the end of the war in March 1815, only fifty-seven vessels were registered in Salem, compared with 250 ten years earlier. Clearly, Salem had begun a long and steady decline that would end in the 1870s with the closing of the last merchant house, of Silsbee and Stone.

By 1850, when Nathaniel Hawthorne wrote the introductory essay to *The Scarlet Letter*, entitled "The Custom-House," Salem's waterfront was in virtual decay. The Naumkeag Steam Cotton Company by then occupied the bank across the South River Channel from Union Wharf. Gone from Stage Point was Enos Brigg's Shipyard, where some of Salem's greatest vessels had been launched. The railroad had come to Salem, and the city had begun to fill in the "inner harbor" of the South River where Puritan shallops and boatyards had once been seen. The warehouses on Front Street and Derby Street and along Derby's Wharf were standing, but idle and often empty. The East Indiamen no longer off-loaded cargoes of tea, pepper, spices, silk, and India cotton goods. Instead, lumber schooners deposited firewood and milled boards at dockside lumberyards, coal barges brought fuel to the waterfront factories and mills, and tanneries were supplied with cargoes of raw cotton and hides. Hawthorne mourned the slow death of the port and hearkened back to the days of "King Derby," when his father and grandfather had sailed Salem vessels to the farthest ports of the rich East.

Derby Wharf, half a mile long and two centuries from its heyday. (Jim McAllister)

T. H. Matteson, The Trial of George Jacobs. *(Peabody Essex Museum)*

The Witchcraft Trials of 1692

Salem Witchcraft! Few subjects in American history have so captivated popular attention and resulted in the use of more printers' ink than the hunt for and execution of witches in 1692 Massachusetts. Back in 1831 Charles W. Upham, the junior pastor of the First Church in Salem, who would eventually serve as Salem's mayor, a representative in the U.S. Congress, and author of the definitive nineteenth-century book on the witchcraft hysteria, wrote of Salem: "The historian would find a great amount and variety of material in the annals of this town—greater perhaps, than in any other of its size in the country. But there is one chapter in our history of preeminent interest and importance. The witchcraft delusion of 1692 has attracted universal attention for the last century, and will, in all coming ages, render the name of Salem notable throughout the world."

How correct Upham was. Yet what is it that gives this topic such a life of its own? Part of the answer rests with the fascination most humans have with topics dabbling in the unknown, the unseen, the supernatural. The existence of a literal devil and his human witch cohorts is beyond the normal realm of historical verification. The titillation of a subject that brings into play even the faintest possibility of supernatural and diabolical presence, and historical figures who act on a belief in this invisible part of the universe, is a spice seldom found within history texts. The surviving documents associated with the Salem witchcraft trials are filled with dramatic depositions sworn to by neighbors, horrendous and scary fits exhibited by young girls, unbelievable, self-incriminating declarations mouthed by confessing witches, and staunch statements of innocence proclaimed by victims awaiting an excruciating death by strangulation from a rope necklace. The drama of these witch-related events is palpable. It entices our attention and interest, while it raises intriguing questions. Did the Massachusetts Puritans really believe these witch stories, or were they part of a now-obscure conspiracy of some kind? What would we have done if confronted by such accusations of witchcraft?

Fascination with these strange occurrences extends beyond the general public. Almost since the last witch victim was cut down from the gallows, numerous scholars have explored the rich body of primary sources related to the 1692 witch phenomena. They attempt to discover new meaning and reach new understanding about the causes of the accusations and trials.

In our own times the words "Salem witch hunt" have been seared into our nation's psyche. They now

Witch Trial Sites in Danvers

1. Salem Village Parsonage (Rear 67 Centre Street) Archaeological site of the family home of the Rev. Samuel Parris.

2. Rebecca Nurse Homestead (149 Pine Street) House occupied by one of the victims. Also on the grounds is a replica of the old Salem Village Meetinghouse.

3. Witchcraft Victims' Memorial (176 Hobart Street) Dedicated in 1992. Directly opposite is the site of the original Salem Village Meetinghouse.

4. Danvers Archival Center (In Peabody Institute Library, 15 Sylvan Street) An important repository of witchcraft volumes.

serve as a catchphrase used by social, cultural, and political commentators when attempting to describe confrontations in which a group of people unreasonably or prejudicially accuses another of some corrupting, societal sin. The Salem witchcraft trials have become a familiar part of our shared American memory.

Puritans in the New World

The city that the world now knows as Salem, Massachusetts, was in the first years of the seventeenth century a small speck on the rugged stretch of land bordering the Atlantic Ocean and inhabited by aboriginal natives. This coastal area was occasionally visited by adventurous European sailors and explorers. A few brave souls established scattered seasonal stations to take advantage of the rich coastal fishing waters.

The first Europeans actually to settle at what became known as Salem were led by Roger Conant. In 1627 Conant moved a small band of settlers south from a failing fishing station at Gloucester to the more attractive Naumkeag peninsula. This group of families, later to be known as the "Old Planters," arrived at Naumkeag (an Indian word meaning "fishing place") and established a fragile squatters' settlement.

Meanwhile, back in England that same year, a group of gentlemen gathered themselves into a mercantile association known as the Massachusetts Bay Company. They obtained from King Charles I a charter for settling territory in New England. This charter would allow the company to govern itself and to "establish all manner of wholesome and reasonable orders, laws, etc., not contrary to the law of this our realm of England."

The stockholders of the Massachusetts Bay Company were predominantly sincere and sober adherents of a branch of the English church known as the Puritans. Though these believers did not reject the official Church of England, as did the separatists who settled in Plymouth beginning in 1620, they did reject many trappings of the church, wanting to purify it of "papist" practices and beliefs. These Puritans held to the theological teaching of John Calvin. Their brand of severe Protestantism was rejected, however, by the majority of the English, and the Puritans often found themselves a persecuted minority in England. They therefore viewed a potential New World settlement not simply as a place to exploit riches for profit, but also as a staging area for the creation of a "New Jerusalem." In this refuge they could mold a society based on their interpretation of biblical principles. Indeed, unlike most financiers of exploitative New World ventures, the Massachusetts Bay Company stockholders made commitments to settle eventually in the new territory. They would remain loyal to England but would live as independently as possible from its religious and political interference. They would permanently set-

tle with like-minded people and establish a Puritan commonwealth. True to their beliefs, they would not allow strangers to question or defile the religious truths they knew to be correct and God-inspired.

To lay claim to their new land quickly, the Massachusetts Bay Company selected "a fit instrument to begin this wilderness work, of courage bold." Their choice for leading the scouting expedition was thirty-nine-year-old John Endecott, a brave, impetuous, religious, and austere gentleman. With about seventy other followers, Endecott set sail aboard the *Abigail* on June 20, 1628, for the new territory. They landed at Naumkeag on September 6 after an Atlantic crossing of some eighty days. Endecott established a permanent settlement and soon changed the name of this new community from Naumkeag to the Hebrew word for "peace"—Salem. He had firmly planted an Anglo-American Puritan foothold in the New World and in history.

Within two years, John Winthrop, the elected governor of the Massachusetts Bay Company, brought himself, the self-governing company charter, and a large contingent of settlers, including ministers, indentured servants, women, and children, from England to Salem. Soon, however, Winthrop moved fifteen miles south, establishing the capital of the new Puritan colony at the peninsula the settlers named Boston. During the next decade, a "Great Migration" crossed the Atlantic to help establish the new Puritan commonwealth. These pioneers slowly moved inland, creating new townships and establishing churches. They governed themselves accord-

> Endecott established a permanent settlement and soon changed the name of this new community from Naumkeag to the Hebrew word for "peace"—Salem.

ing to their understanding of God's law and English tradition.

Though zealous to secure their own religious freedom, the Puritans pounced on anyone preaching a doctrine contrary to theirs. Thus theological troublemakers who arose within their midst were banished, including Roger Williams, the eventual founder of Rhode Island, and Anne Hutchinson, the independent religious thinker. Members of the Society of Friends, an English proselytizing sect popularly known as the Quakers, were violently persecuted during the 1650s. Monetary fines, banishments, whippings, cutting off of ears, brandings, and public hangings were frequently used by the Puritans to control these anathematized pests.

> These pioneers slowly moved inland, creating new townships and establishing churches.

Salem Village

As decades passed and many of the first settlers died off, some of the fervent religious zeal of those first-generation adventurers waned. The second and third generations of Puritan inhabitants settled into the hard but often rewarding rhythm of daily life. As the coastal land in Salem Town was quickly portioned out, newly arriving settlers found it necessary to seek unoccupied territory further inland. In about 1637 a small group of families moved five to ten miles west of Salem Center, finding this interior land more suitable for agriculture than the land located close to the rocky seacoast. Predominantly farmers, these settlers established well-regulated homesteads and began referring to this western territory as Salem Village. Over the years these yeoman families found less and less in common with the more mercantile inhabitants of Salem Town and began to petition for their own interests. In most Puritan communities it was traditional that, when a significant local minority settled an outlying area of the original community, the outlying area was allowed independence. In Salem, however, matters proceeded differently. Though the village began petitioning as early as 1667, the town would not concede the village its governmental independence for an incredible eighty-five years.

This seeming subjugation of Salem Village by Salem Town caused ill feeling and obstinate uncooperativeness to fester between the two areas. As a gesture of compromise, in 1672 the town did allow the village to establish a parish within the Salem town system. The villagers were allowed to build their own meetinghouse, hire a minister to preach among them, and tax themselves for their ecclesiastical maintenance. If villagers desired covenant church membership and participation in the sacraments, however, they still needed to attend the Salem mother church.

Rather than unifying the villagers, the long-awaited establishment of a parish seemed only to foster dissension. The short tenures of the first three village preachers from 1672 to 1688 were marked by frequent clashes between village factions supporting or objecting to the minister. The lack of traditional institutions in Salem Village, as well as its inability to establish consensus in running its own parish affairs, became well known throughout the colony. Though many of the village's problems were homegrown, Salem Town shared much of the blame for them through its heavy-handed dealings with Salem Village.

The Rebecca Nurse homestead in Salem Village (now Danvers), one of the homes built by the settlers who moved inland from Salem Town. (Richard B. Trask)

In 1689 a glimmer of hope appeared. The villagers made an unusual show of unity to petition for an independent, full-covenant church completely separate from the Salem mother church. The Salem church acquiesced, and in November 1689 the Church of Christ at Salem Village was established with a new minister, the Reverend Mr. Samuel Parris, ordained as its spiritual leader.

Within two years, however, the village had backslid into intense conflict between supporters and detractors of Rev. Parris. He was a strong-willed man who demanded more from his parish and church than many believed he needed or deserved. By late 1691 the minister found himself in a precarious position. Though he enjoyed the support of most of the covenanted church members, this group was a minority in the village. Parris was not supported by the newly elected Village Committee, the five-man group responsible for collecting the minister's salary. By the beginning of 1692, Salem Village, with a population of some 550 souls housed within ninety homesteads scattered throughout nineteen square miles of territory, was truly a community in crisis. The only established institution within the village was engaged in a divisive power struggle. And at that point in time strange occurrences began to take place at the minister's parsonage.

Witch hunts elsewhere

During the seventeenth century the average Englishman believed in the existence of a literal devil who continually intervened on earth, attempting to bring ruin upon the godly. Assisting the devil in his diabolical efforts were mortals who had made personal pacts to serve him in exchange for special favors. These witches, who tended to be women but on occasion could also be males, allegedly brought all manner of evil upon other mortals and their possessions. Considered an "exceptional and secret crime," witchcraft was often prosecuted with little regard for normal legal safeguards. Tests, both physical and mental, as well as torture were considered proper tools in the discovery of the crime of witchcraft.

Accusations of witchcraft in England had lagged behind the massive witch hunts so prevalent on the European continent during the fifteenth through seventeenth centuries. Beginning in the sixteenth century, however, witch hunts multiplied in England. A famous case in Chelmsford, England, in 1566, during which three women were tried and hanged for bewitching village children, was widely reported. Another notorious witch trial was played out at Bury St. Edmunds in 1682. During the English Civil War of the 1640s, witch hunts and persecutions rose to an all-time high. About two hundred people were put to death as witches. Though by the late seventeenth century many English scholars were debating the existence of witches, the general population continued to believe that undiscovered witchcraft was the true cause of much strife and difficulty.

New England was not immune to perceived attacks by Satan. Massachusetts Puritans believed that the "Old Deluder" was hard at work attempting to overthrow their model Puritan commonwealth. Prior to 1692, over

> The average Englishman believed in the existence of a literal devil who continually intervened on earth.

ninety witch accusations had been made, including several famous cases such as the affliction of John Goodwin's children in Boston in 1688, held to be perpetrated by an Irish woman named Mary Glover. The Reverend Cotton Mather of Boston reported this and other cases in a widely known work published in 1689, entitled *Memorable Providences, Relating to Witchcrafts and Possessions.*

The first outbreak

In early 1692 in little Salem Village, the Reverend Samuel Parris's nine-year-old daughter Elizabeth, his twelve-year-old niece Abigail Williams, and other neighborhood girls including twelve-year-old Ann Putnam began to experience unusual and frightening fits. According to one eyewitness, "These children were bitten and pinched by invisible agents; their armes, necks, and backs turned this way and that way. . . . Sometimes they were taken dumb, their mouths stopped, their throats choked, their limbs wracked and tormented so as might move an heart of stone." The anxious parents of these seemingly tormented girls attempted to discover the cause of their dis-

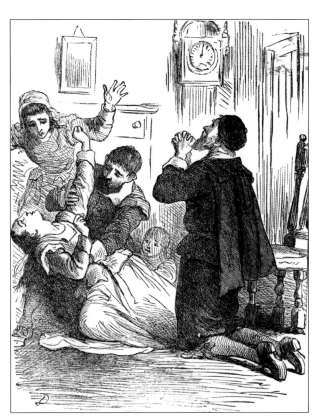

Nineteenth-century print "Deliverance from Witchcraft" shows minister praying over stricken girl—and an anachronistic grandfather clock. (Danvers Archival Center)

tress. Under Rev. Parris's guidance, prayer meetings were held with the children in attendance. The adults also held private fasts and called upon other ministers in the area to visit and pray over the girls.

Finally a village doctor named William Griggs was asked to examine the girls. His diagnosis concluded that these children were victims of an evil hand. Once it was recognized that these fits were not epileptic-like seizures or anything known to nature and that these afflictions were dangerously spreading to other children, firm action was required. The girls were put upon by the adults to name who afflicted them so violently. For now-obscure reasons and undoubtedly under heavy adult pressure, the girls finally named three women: Rev. Parris's Indian slave, Tituba; a destitute thirty-nine-year-old woman of ill repute and acid tongue named Sarah Good; and Sarah Osburn, a sickly woman whose unsavory marital past was the occasion for much local gossip. According to the girls, these women's spectres, invisible to all but the girls themselves, were tormenting them. These three women of low standing and with problematic backgrounds are typical of women accused during seventeenth-century witch hunts.

Neighbors swore out complaints against these women, and John Hathorne and Jonathan Corwin, two prominent Salem citizens who served in the colony as members of the ruling-class Court of Assistants, issued arrest warrants. On March 1, 1692, Hathorne and Corwin traveled from Salem Town to Salem Village to conduct an examination of these three suspects.

Sarah Good and Sarah Osburn were separately examined at the village meetinghouse. As the accused answered the questions put to them by the Salem magistrates, the "afflicted" girls displayed publicly and loudly their horrific fits. Their torments amazed and frightened the large audience watching the examination. To all present, it appeared obvious that these girls were victims of the women's vile witchcraft. Though Good and Osburn attempted to protest their own innocence, Tituba, when examined, unraveled a frightful confession of an actual meeting with the devil. He told her to hurt the children. Tituba also indicated that, besides the three under arrest, other undiscovered witches lurked in the neighborhood. The self-incriminating testimony of Tituba and the apparent sincerity of her words left few doubting that they were witnessing a diabolical conspiracy between the devil and his witch assistants. This evidence was enough for the magistrates, and the three women were jailed to await a formal trial.

Instead of cooling the villagers' anxiety about witchcraft, the examinations of these three women only fueled their fear. A confessed witch, two lying accomplices, and

> "As to this thing, I am Innocent as the child unborne."
> (Rebecca Nurse)

others as yet unknown were in league with the devil and actively attacking the village. The girls were none the better for the discovery of these three witches, and soon they were joined in their torments by other afflicted persons including several older women.

Soon the afflicted ones began to accuse others, but not just villagers of ill repute. By late March, Martha Cory, a village church member in good standing, had been accused, examined, and jailed. Perhaps the most famous of the soon to be 150 witch suspects of 1692 was seventy-one-year-old Rebecca Nurse. In 1678 Francis Nurse, a tray maker by trade, moved with his wife, Rebecca, and their many children from Salem Town to a three-hundred-acre homestead in Salem Village. Rebecca was a covenant member of the Salem Town church, though she generally attended the closer village meetinghouse. She was known for her piety and devotion to God. Thus it was a shock to many when, on March 19, 1692, Rebecca's spectre was named as one of their torturers by some of the bewitched girls. When told she was being spoken against by several of the afflicted girls, Nurse declared, "Well, if it be soe, ye will of the Lord be done." Then after a few moments of amazed disbelief, she asked, "As to this thing, I am Innocent as the child unborne, but seurly what sine hath God found out in me unrepented of that he should Lay such an Affliction upon me In my old Age?"

On March 23 a formal complaint was issued against Rebecca Nurse for "haveing donne Much hurt and Injury to the Bodys of Ann Putnam the wife of Thomas Putnam of Salem Village, Ann Putnam ye daufter of Said

The "Witch House," 310½ Essex Street, owned by witch trials judge Jonathan Corwin. (Jim McAllister)

Court officials look for so-called witch marks in T. H. Matteson's The Examination of a Witch. *(Peabody Essex Museum)*

Thomas Putnam, and Abigail Williams." On March 24, Nurse was brought to the crowded village meetinghouse for examination. Asked by John Hathorne how she responded to the women's accusation, Nurse stated, "I can say before my Eternal father I am innocent, and God will clear my innocency." Hathorne, cognizant that Nurse was a full church member and not the type traditionally to be in league with the devil, replied, "Here is never a one in the Assembly but desires it, but if you be guilty Pray God discover you." Suddenly the afflicted persons began falling into terrifying fits, and the examination turned into pandemonium. The testimony of middle-aged Ann Putnam, which stated that the shape of Nurse had come to her home and almost killed her, was read. Nurse could offer only this defense: "I cannot help it, the Devil may appear in my shape." There was little the accused could do to defend themselves against invisible shapes and very visible accusers.

> Suddenly the afflicted persons began falling into terrifying fits, and the examination turned into pandemonium.

Court of Oyer and Terminer

The witch troubles began spreading beyond the confines of Salem Village. During April and May, scores of others were accused and thrown in jail. The hysteria spread throughout Salem, Essex County, and much of eastern Massachusetts. Some of the accused, such as John Alden, Jr., of Boston and Philip English of Salem, were influential and wealthy men; others, such as Wilmot Reed of Marblehead and Bridget Bishop of Salem, had been previously suspected of practicing witchcraft.

On May 14, 1692, a new governor, Sir William Phips, arrived from England. Phips, appointed by King William and Queen Mary, had been issued a new charter for the governance of Massachusetts. For many months prior to his arrival, there was no legally constituted government. Upon landing, Phips found himself facing a crisis: the jails were filled with suspected witches. It would be some time before elections and a new judiciary system could be established, so Phips found himself in a quandary. The governor was counseled to set up a special emergency Court of Oyer and Terminer, an English legal measure meant to deal with instances of social disorder—to hear, determine, and dispose of the backlog of cases. Within two weeks Phips appointed a special court to handle these cases, with the dour deputy governor William Stoughton as chief justice and seven other prominent colonists sitting with him. The sessions would take place in Salem rather than Boston and would be run according to English law and precedent relating to witchcraft cases. Stoughton was a determined man who constructed the court according to his own dictates of propriety. Although some people, including several influential ministers, questioned the validity of spectral evidence, Stoughton seemed sure that it was sound. He felt that God would not allow an innocent person's spectre to be used for diabolical purposes.

On June 2, 1692, the special court was ready to hear its first case. Bridget Bishop of Salem, who had been jailed since her preliminary examination on April 19, was indicted. About sixty years old, Bishop had been married to three men, including Thomas Oliver, who had died in 1679. Edward Bishop, a Salem sawyer, was now living with Bishop at the former Oliver house on

Witch Trial Sites in Salem

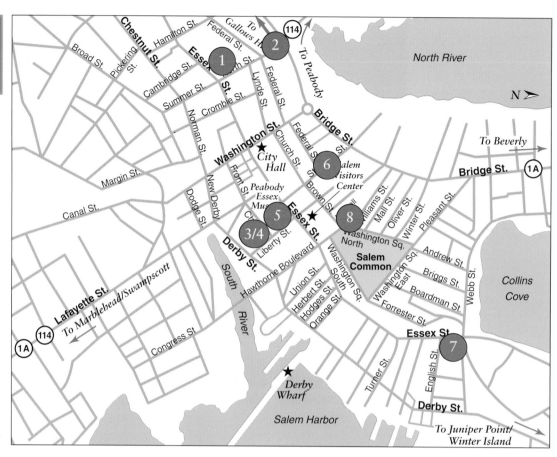

1. Jonathan Corwin House ("The Witch House") (310½ Essex Street) Ironically, this is the only house still standing in Salem with any direct connection to the witch trials. It was the home of magistrate Jonathan Corwin who examined and sentenced suspected witches.

2. Gallows Hill Park So long buried was Salem's memory of the witch trials that no one is entirely sure where the accused witches were executed. The city maintains a park at the most likely site, above the area known as "Blubber Hollow."

3. Old Burying Point (Charter Street) The oldest cemetery in Salem contains the gravestone of witch trials judge John Hathorne, an ancestor of Nathaniel Hawthorne.

4. Salem Witch Trials Memorial (Charter Street) Erected next to the seventeenth-century Burying Point, the memorial was dedicated to the witch trial victims on August 5, 1992, during the tercentenary.

5. Peabody Essex Museum (East India Square) Largest collection of documents and artifacts related to the witch trials.

6. Site of Salem Gaol (On Prison Lane, now St. Peter Street near Federal Street) This is where accused witches were held while awaiting trial and, in the case of the unfortunate, death. Giles Corey was tortured and died on the grounds.

7. Site of Philip English House At the head of what is now English Street, this was where Philip English, the wealthiest man in Salem, lived in 1692 when he and his wife Mary were accused of witchcraft.

8. Salem Witch Museum (19½ Washington Square) The oldest modern-day attraction dedicated to the witch trials, the museum offers a multimedia presentation in the former Second Church building. A statue of Salem founder Roger Conant stands outside.

what is now Church Street. Bridget's trial took place close by, at the Salem Townhouse located in the middle of present-day Washington Street, about opposite Salem City Hall. Hers was the ideal test case for the court. Of questionable character, Bridget had previously been indicted for lying and stealing and in 1680 on charges of witchcraft. In addition to the testimonies of many girls that her spectre had afflicted them during her April examination, Bishop had been caught in several lies during that questioning. While she was in prison, a "witch mark" had been discovered upon Bishop's body. The court-appointed examiners noted that it had disappeared only hours later. A number of men testified that Bishop's spectre had plagued them

The "Great House" of Philip English. (Danvers Archival Center)

in the past. Two men testified to having found poppets, dolls made of rags and stuck with pins, undoubtedly the tools of witchcraft, in the cellar of the house in which she had once lived. A confessed witch named Deliverance Hobbs gave testimony that Bishop was a witch and had even helped to distribute sacraments at a witches' Sabbat. With all this evidence reported against her, the jury impaneled by the court was convinced that the Salem woman was guilty. On June 8, 1692, Judge Stoughton signed her execution warrant, and Bishop was hanged two days later in that section of Salem for-

ever referred to as Gallows Hill, near the present-day Proctor Street.

Philip and Mary English

Although Bridget Bishop could be considered representative of the type of woman accused during the English witch-hunt outbreaks of the sixteenth and seventeenth centuries, the Salem accusations soon broke the typical mold. Two of the most socially prominent of the accused were Philip and Mary English of Salem Town. Born on the Isle of Jersey off the English coast in 1651, Philipe L'Anglois immigrated to New England and in 1674 married Mary Holingworth, a member of a wealthy Salem merchant family. Anglicizing his name, Philip quickly prospered in America so that by 1692 he was the richest man in Salem and one of the wealthiest in New England. He owned numerous town properties, a wharf, and twenty-one vessels that traded with England and the Continent. The family lived near the waterfront in a dwelling known as the "Great House," the grandest home in all of Salem. The house was at the head of what is now English Street, not far from Collins Cove. In early March 1692, English was elected a selectman of the town, and his wealth and standing in the community seemed firm.

An accused witch being led to the gallows. (Danvers Archival Center)

Yet the English family was not universally loved. Mrs. English had a reputation for flaunting her position in life. Many Salemites also resented how Philip frequently sued in court to settle even the slightest dispute. His non-native, French customs were also looked upon with suspicion, and his good fortune was undoubtedly the subject of some local jealousy.

On April 21, 1692, a complaint was sworn against Mary English for afflicting Salem Village girls Mercy Lewis, Ann Putnam, and Mary Walcott. According to tradition in the English family, the county sheriff arrived with the warrant for Mary's arrest at the family mansion after 11:00 P.M. Mary instructed the court officer that it was too late for such business, as she had already retired for the night, and that he should return in the morning after breakfast.

Witch trials judge William Stoughton.
(Danvers Archival Center)

The following day Mrs. English was brought to Salem Village and questioned by magistrates Hathorne and Corwin. Little documentation survives regarding her case, though an indictment is preserved recounting that during her examination Mrs. English "Tortured afflicted Consumed Pined Wasted and Tormented" seventeen-year-old Elizabeth Hubbard. Mary was held over and eventually sent to prison in Boston.

By May 31, Philip had also been accused, arrested, examined, and imprisoned. Among the charges laid against him was the murder by witchcraft of at least one man. Salem sheriff George Corwin seized much of the Englishes' movable property amounting to 1,500 pounds in value. Philip would never be able to reclaim a just settlement against his property losses, though as the Court of Oyer and Terminer began condemning persons to the gallows, the loss of his property became of less concern than the potential loss of his and his wife's lives.

During June the couple was kept in prison in Boston. Given their upper-class status, the two prisoners were granted certain privileges not allowed poorer witch suspects, including freedom of the town during daylight hours. In early August the couple attended services at Boston's First Church. Rev. Joshua Moodey, a friend of the Englishes and critic of the witch court proceedings, used as his sermon text a passage from the Gospel of Saint Matthew, urging, "If they persecute you in one city, flee to another." The message was received, and with the urging and assistance of other Boston friends, as well as their own deep pockets, Philip and Mary escaped from their genteel confinement in Boston, finding protection in New York with Governor Benjamin Fletcher. Witch

Gallows Hill. (Jim McAllister)

accusations were indeed made in 1692 against not only the lowly and powerless, but also against rich and influential people like Philip and Mary English. But the powerful victims had the resources and connections to escape.

Following Bridget Bishop's trial, misgivings had surfaced about the acceptability of some of the evidence. The court sought advice from leading ministers to clarify what could be considered valid proofs when confronting a secret crime such as witchcraft. Rev. Cotton Mather of Boston drafted the ministers' reply, recommending that the proceedings be mixed with tenderness for those accused who formerly had "an unblemished reputation." Spectral evidence should be treated carefully, since a demon may "by God's permission, appear even to ill purposes in the shape of an innocent, yea, and a virtuous man." Yet the document also pointed out the importance of the court's mandate to "detect the abominable witchcrafts." With the ministers' advice as guide, the court resumed its work in late June.

A rash of executions

Rebecca Nurse had been previously indicted by the grand jury, and her formal trial took place on June 28. Much of the evidence in her case was spectral in nature, and members of the jury, probably guided by the ministers' advice, were impressed by neighbors' petitions in her favor and the fact that she had long been a full covenant church member in Salem. Following deliberations, the jury found her not guilty. When they informed the court of their verdict, hysteria, the likes of which no one expected, broke out. The afflicted girls present in the courtroom, who had been relatively quiet during the trial, now were convulsed into almost unbelievable fits that frightened and confused nearly everyone. It appeared that witchcraft was at work in this very room. Judge Stoughton quizzed the jury, asking whether they had considered some seemingly self-incriminating testimony made by Nurse. When the old woman did not explain herself, the jury was instructed to reconsider the evidence. They retired and came back with a new verdict of guilty.

Although Nurse's children made valiant efforts to obtain a reprieve and save her life, it was to no avail. The court's vote of doom was coupled with another crushing blow for this frail old matriarch. On July 3 Nurse was carried from jail to the Salem church located at the southeast corner of the intersection of modern-day Washington and Essex Streets. Her minister wrote in the church record book what transpired there at the meetinghouse filled with Sabbath worshipers: "After the Sacrament the Elders propounded to the Church, and it was by a unanimous vote consented to, that our sister Nurse being a convicted witch by the court and condemned to dy, should be Excommunicated, which was accordingly done in the Afternoon, she being present."

On Tuesday, July 19, 1692, Rebecca, along with four other convicted witches, was executed by hanging at Gallows Hill. Rebecca's children later secretly retrieved their mother's lifeless body, bore it to her beloved home-

> "But such was the darkness of that day, the tortures and lamentations of the afflicted, and the power of former presidents [precedents], that we walked in the clouds, and could not see our way."
> (Rev. John Hale)

stead, and placed it in the family burial ground. Today, a few hundred feet down an ancient cart path from the saltbox-style Nurse house located at 149 Pine Street in Danvers, a granite memorial obelisk to Rebecca stands among the family graves. Nearby is another marker inscribed with the names of the neighbors who signed a petition in Rebecca's favor.

Two other residents of Salem Town proper, besides Bridget Bishop, were counted among the nineteen executed witches of 1692. Of Alice Parker, little background information survives. She was the wife of John Parker, a Salem fisherman who lived off present-day Derby Street on property now owned by the New England Power Company. Alice Parker was complained against on May 12, 1692, along with another Salemite, Ann Pudeator. Pudeator was about sixty years old in 1692 and the widow of two Salem husbands, the latter being Jacob Pudeator, who had died in 1682. Widow Pudeator lived on her husband's estate on the north side of the Common, near what is now Washington Square North. She had several children living outside Salem and some years previously had been accused of witchcraft. Though nothing seems to have come of that previous accusation, people's memories kept such stories alive.

Marshal George Herrick arrested both women under a warrant signed by John Hathorne and Jonathan Corwin on the charge of "sundry acts of witchcrafts by them committed." Though Pudeator's original examination is no longer extant, there is a record of Parker's questioning. Mary Warren, a twenty-year-old servant girl, accused Parker of a number of acts of witchcraft,

> The Court of Oyer and Terminer heard witchcraft cases during sessions in June, July, and August.

including bewitching several mariners to death and bringing a poppet to Warren, urging her to run a needle into it, thereby assisting her in serving the devil. Parker would not confess to any of this and instead proffered that "she wished God would open the Earth and swallow her up presently, if one word of this was true and make her an Example to others." Such an oath challenge was quickly swept aside as Warren suddenly fell into terrifying fits. Viewers agreed that these were obviously the result of Parker's diabolical actions. Parker and Pudeator were held for trial.

In preparation for trial, Pudeator was brought from Boston prison and confined to the Salem gaol (jail) on Prison Lane, now St. Peter Street near Federal Street. She was examined again by local magistrates on July 2 at the Thomas Beadle Tavern located on present-day Essex Street, near Daniels Street. Sarah Churchill, one of the young afflicted servant girls, testified that Pudeator forced her to put her name in the devil's book. Soon most of the afflicted group present, including Ann Putnam, Elizabeth Hubbard, and Mary Walcott, also showed signs of being attacked by Pudeator's invisible spectre.

The Court of Oyer and Terminer heard witchcraft cases during sessions in June, July, and August. They again gathered at the second-floor court at the Salem Townhouse in early September. The Grand Jury of Inquest heard testimony and considered sworn depositions concerning both of the Salem women. The evidence presented to them in these and most other cases fell into two broad categories: (1) statements of witchcraft being committed upon the group of afflicted persons during preliminary examinations of suspected witches, and (2) depositions by persons who claimed evidences of witchcraft committed on them or their family and friends. This latter evidence was recollected many months or years after the incidents had supposedly taken place. The Salem women, along with several others, were indicted on the capital charge of witchcraft. Pleading not guilty, they were put to a swift jury trial. Both Pudeator and Parker maintained their innocence, but these simple women could not present evidence to counter the adverse depositions and testimonies put forth in court. They were tried, found guilty, and condemned to hang in their own town.

Not long before her execution, Pudeator petitioned the court, stating that several of those who testified against her gave testimony "altogether false & untrue," and begging "that my life may not be taken away by such false Evidence and witnesses as these." She proclaimed her innocence to the charges of witchcraft "as will be known to men and angells at the great day of Judgment." Her petition caused not a ripple

of comment by the court. On September 22, 1692, the last and largest set of executions took place. Along with Martha Cory of Salem Village, Pudeator, Parker, and five others had their lives snuffed out by rope strangulation. By September's end, the Court of Oyer and Terminer had sent nineteen men and women to the gallows and had condemned five others. Another person, Giles Cory, husband of Martha, was brutally tortured at Salem gaol, dying on September 19, one day after the Salem church, where he was a covenant member, had excommunicated him.

Return of conscience

During the eight months of witchcraft accusations in 1692, over forty persons confessed to being witches. This was the best way, practically speaking, to buy time. A confession temporarily forestalled the legal process, since confessed witches no longer posed an immediate danger to the population. It soon became evident that, according to the workings of the system, an accused witch who did not confess was speedily tried, found guilty, and hanged. For any person motivated pri-

Title page of Increase Mather's Cases of Conscience *(1693), which was instrumental in bringing the witch delusion to an end. (Danvers Archival Center)*

Witchcraft Victims' Memorial, 176 Hobart Street, Danvers. (Richard B. Trask)

marily by the yen to live, the necessary course of action was obvious.

Those who had the spirit to declare their innocence were the only ones condemned and killed. That many of them were flawed or failed individuals makes their courage all the more impressive. They share a common bond of standing up for the truth, at the ultimate cost. Their strength of character is well expressed in the words of George Jacobs, Sr., an old yeoman who lived in the outlying North Fields section of Salem. In the statement he offered when accused of practicing witchcraft, he said, "Well! Burn me or hang me, I will stand in the truth of Christ, I know nothing of it." These victims of the witch hunt valued truth, regardless of the consequences.

> "It were better that ten suspected witches should escape than one innocent person should be condemned."
> (Increase Mather)

The court adjourned in September, intending to resume in October. But dissatisfaction over the entire witchcraft matter was festering. In June, Judge Nathaniel Saltonstall had quit the court, "very much Dissatisfied with the proceedings of it." He had been replaced by Jonathan Corwin. In the fall Rev. Samuel Willard of Boston, who had known a number of the accused, including the Englishes, as well as several of the judges, anonymously circulated a pamphlet denouncing the use of spectral evidence in court and calling the afflicted accusers "scandalous persons, liars, and loose in their conversation." Many thought that the accusations had become too broad in scope and included persons too spotless to possibly be in collusion with the devil. Rev. Increase Mather, the father of Cotton Mather, wrote a tract in October that received much credence. Titled

Cases of Conscience Concerning Evil Spirits Personating Men, the booklet questioned much of the evidence allowed by the court, though without impeaching the good intentions of the court itself. Mather firmly declared, "It were better that ten suspected witches should escape than one innocent person should be condemned."

With public opinion turning and with many theological lights reshaping, if not completely altering, their opinion, Governor Phips finally took the initiative and allowed no further jail committals. By late October, the Court of Oyer and Terminer was abandoned.

When the new Superior Court of Judicature was established, it became the venue for clearing up the remaining witch cases. Though William Stoughton continued to serve as the court's chief justice, spectral evidence was no longer allowed. Cases began to be heard on January 3, 1693, with most of them being thrown out by the grand juries. The five persons condemned in the September sitting by the old court were given a reprieve by the governor. In May the governor, wanting to end this unhappy and controversial episode, proclaimed a "general jail delivery of pardon."

With the waning of the witch persecution, Philip and Mary English returned to Salem in 1693 from their New York refuge. They attempted to put their lives back in order. Tragically, Mary died in 1694, the result of childbirth complicated by consumption contracted during her Boston imprisonment. Philip, never able to recover his pre-1692 financial standing, lived till 1736. Several years prior to his death he assisted in founding St. Peter's

Church, an Anglican church established amidst old Puritan Salem.

The roaring attack upon Salem Village and Massachusetts purportedly brought on by the devil and an army of witches eventually exhausted those caught up in it. Normal life in many communities was put on hold for months, and those hundreds of families directly involved experienced terrible trauma. The maelstrom finally ran out of energy when first cautious and then decisive complaints against the court were expressed by members of the religious and governing classes. It would be years before some of the accused or their surviving families would obtain legal apologies and some remuneration for their losses. The names of other victims would not be cleared for hundreds of years until votes and proclamations would acknowledge the false charges made against them. Some prosecutors, including William Stoughton, would never admit to having made gross mistakes. Still others, including the foreman and jury that had condemned Rebecca Nurse, attempted sincere apologies. As Rev. John Hale of Beverly would write several years following the witch times, "But such was the darkness of that day, the tortures and lamentations of the afflicted,

Roses left in memory of Rebecca Nurse at the Salem Witchcraft Memorial. (Jim McAllister)

and the power of former presidents [precedents], that we walked in the clouds, and could not see our way."

Scores of years would pass before memories of suffering, fear, guilt, and the perpetrators' lack of charity would subside. In Salem, the town of peace, where the first settlers arrived to establish a godly homeland, something terrible had happened. Every legal, ecclesiastical, and familial safeguard had failed. The godly took this proof of their frailty to heart and resolved never again to visit such a sin upon themselves. The raw, open wounds of the witchcraft era in the Salem and Salem Village communities festered for many generations. Although the villagers attempted to forget, or at least to keep silent about 1692, outsiders were fascinated. Historians began writing accounts of it. In 1752 Salem Village finally became independent and was given a new name, Danvers, helping somewhat to dissociate it from its notorious past. Salem Town, later a city, was always the more heavily populated and cosmopolitan community of the two. In 1692 its citizens had generally escaped the most intimate horrors of the witch events, which had so inundated the Salem Village church and population.

The "Witch City"?

As decades passed, memories and hurts faded. Salem also became renowned for its rich maritime and architectural history and as the home of famed nineteenth-century novelist Nathaniel Hawthorne. Beginning in the late nineteenth century, the Salem community began to capitalize on its witch history. It took on the moniker of "Witch City." Cartoon witches riding broomsticks were replicated on tourist kitsch, publications, signs, and advertisements as the non-threatening symbols of Salem. These harmless, humorous grotesques bear no resemblance to the alleged evildoers feared by the Puritans. To confuse the historical record even further, during the 1980s many believers in pre-Christian wicca—modern-day witches —were drawn to the Salem community to live, worship, and pursue the tourist dollar. They hold yet another definition for the word *witch:* one who does good, according to the dictates of their religion.

In 1992, during the three-hundredth anniversary of the persecution, both Salem and Danvers commemorated the events of 1692 by celebrating those people who had died speaking the truth. Both communities set up active tercentennial committees to face the challenge of treating a difficult, terrible, often media-hyped subject with dignity in a way that acknowledged that even the most horrible historical events can lead to positive developments. On May 9, 1992, the Town of Danvers and on August 5, 1992, the City of Salem dedicated permanent witch victim memorials. Each community came up with a design that expressed its understanding of the 1692 events. During this tercentennial, two lessons for our own times emerged. First, the fact was celebrated that even flawed individuals can in times of profound crisis choose the integrity of truth over life. Second, the story of Salem in 1692 offered a chilling reminder that each generation must confront its share of intolerance and witch hunts with integrity, clear vision, and bravery.

> Cartoon witches riding broomsticks were replicated on tourist kitsch, publications, signs, and advertisements as the nonthreatening symbols of Salem.

The Cook-Oliver House. (Jim McAllister)

The Historic Architecture of Salem

Salem's reputation for outstanding architecture extends throughout the United States and abroad. Of the older, modest-sized East Coast American communities, it exhibits the richest and most comprehensive variety of pre–World War I styles, building types, and construction practices. Because it is relatively small in population, and has not experienced major physical expansion, it has maintained most of its distinguished architectural heritage for us to study and enjoy today. Urban renewal transformed the downtown Essex Street section of the city during the 1970s, but no significant buildings were lost, and the changes only added luster to Salem's historical ambience.

Salem's architectural development has been conditioned by geographical, cultural, and economic factors. The city's proximity to the sea and its astounding success as a pre–Civil War center of international commerce have had a pronounced impact on its building. The fame of Salem's architectural legacy has largely resulted from achievements of the so-called First Period (c. 1626–c. 1715) and the Federal era (c. 1780–c. 1830). The rare genius of the carver, designer, and builder Samuel McIntire is inextricably linked with the city's great Federal mansions, churches, and public structures. Not surprisingly, these two time periods have received the

most attention in the literature treating Salem's architectural history. In more recent years, however, the city's outstanding assemblage of Greek Revival, Victorian Eclectic, and Colonial Revival buildings (c. 1830–c. 1940) has also attracted attention.

First Period Architecture, c. 1626–1725

Appreciators of New England architecture, whether scholars or casual tourists, have long been attracted to the aged, starkly linear appearance of the region's seventeenth- and early-eighteenth-century buildings and to their mysterious lore. They seem to beg for answers about their origins, the people who occupied and used them, and the history with which they have been associated. Eastern Massachusetts possesses New England's largest and richest collection of surviving buildings from this era, and within this region Salem has long been recognized for its outstanding and highly representative houses. No other city or town in New England can lay claim to such superb examples of early residential architecture or to their abundance of rich stories, both documented and passed down by tradition.

Arriving in 1626 and subsequently, Salem's first settlers erected small, simple wooden shelters and houses, conjectural restorations of which may be seen today at

Pioneer Village. (Jim McAllister)

Pioneer Village (1930) in Forest River Park on Salem Harbor. By 1650, there were two basic types of wood-frame residences locally—(1) the two-room, two-story house with end chimney and (2) the four-room, two-story house with center chimney. The latter type was simply an expansion of the former. Salem's two oldest surviving dwellings, the Pickering House (c. 1651) and the Retire Beckett House (c. 1655), initially comprised two rooms in two stories, but ultimately were expanded to twice this size. Several of the city's earliest houses eventually were furnished with rear lean-tos, evidence of which may be seen today in the Gedney House (c. 1656) and the John Ward House (after 1684). Others featured prominent front gables of the kind present in the Ward House and the Jonathan Corwin House (c. 1675). With its striking multigables and expansive floor plan, the Turner House, popularly known as the House of the Seven Gables (1668; c. 1678), illustrates the larger type of First Period residence, of which only a small number remain today in New England.

Salem's seventeenth-century residential structures possessed a natural and plain look, with limited architectural detail. Boxlike in form and protected by moderate- or steep-pitched roofs, these dwellings consisted of meticulously hewn and pegged timber frames handcrafted by skilled artisans and set on basic, rough stone foundations. Chimneys, often massive, were constructed of brick or stone. In virtually all known instances, the main entrance doorways were positioned off center on the long front elevations. Similarly, windows, customarily of the casement type with leaded, diamond-shaped panes, were small and randomly placed in the outer walls. In a number of the city's early houses, the upper floor projected beyond the lower in the front wall, creating an eye-pleasing overhang. Typically the outer walls were surfaced with narrow, unpainted clapboards and displayed simple board trim. Initially inspired by English Elizabethan rural dwellings, these buildings often were later altered in style and decoration to meet changing needs and cultural trends. Consequently, Salem's surviving seventeenth-century houses have undergone varying degrees of historical restoration to return them to their presumed original appearances.

> Since 1651, when the first documented portion was constructed, the Pickering House was lived in by ten successive generations of Pickerings.

The oldest of the city's First Period residences, the Pickering House (18 Broad Street at Pickering Street), although in an excellent state of preservation, has retained intriguing evidence of mid-nineteenth-century modifications in the Gothic Revival style. One of this country's most important surviving seventeenth-century buildings, it bears a remarkable historical legacy. Since about 1651, when the first documented portion was constructed, and until recently, the house was owned and lived in by ten successive generations of Pickerings, thereby making it the oldest house in the United States to be continuously occupied by a single family. Surely the best-known family member to have lived there was Colonel Timothy Pickering, an aide to General George Washington during the Revolutionary War and a cabinet member during the presidential administrations of Washington and John Adams.

Like the few remaining dwellings of its period and region, the Pickering House evolved over many years.

Pickering House, 18 Broad Street. (Jim McAllister)

Architectural historian Abbott Lowell Cummings, in his book *The Framed Houses of Massachusetts Bay* (1979), has traced the development of the building. The oldest part of the house (a two-story, single-room plan with entry) is believed to have been erected by John Pickering, Jr., a carpenter by trade. In about 1671 the second John Pickering doubled the size of the house to the west (the left side facing Broad Street). Then, under the ownership of Deacon Timothy Pickering in 1751, the house was raised to two stories above a lean-to in the rear, as it may be viewed today. The Gothic details on the front facade, as well as the intriguing cutout front fence and adjacent barn, date from 1841. The two-story clapboarded ell to the rear was added in 1904. Although the Pickering House is hardly a pure example of First Period New England residential architecture, it is highly provocative aesthetically, and in its modified form, it tells us much about an important facet of mid-Victorian cultural taste.

The John Ward House (Brown Street opposite Howard Street on the grounds of the Peabody Essex Museum) has been widely discussed in numerous publications and is generally regarded as one of New England's finest wood-frame-and-clapboard seventeenth-century dwellings. Originally situated nearby at 38 St. Peter Street, it was acquired by the Essex Institute in 1910 and moved to its present site and restored over the next two years under the direction of the distinguished historian and preservationist George Frances Dow. This building dates from no earlier than December 1684 when the land upon which it initially stood was purchased by John Ward, a local currier.

Like the Pickering before it, the Ward House evolved in distinct stages. The first phase (the south half of the present structure) consisted of a one-room plan (the parlor with chamber above, a large brick chimney, porch and stairwell), and featured a cross gable and second-story overhangs both on the front and the south end. As is the case today, the roof was steep-pitched, and dark-stained clapboards covered the outer wall surfaces. By 1732, after Ward's death, the house was doubled in size (the north half was added) so that the front elevation possessed two matching cross gables. At the same time a lean-to was attached in the rear. Today, during open hours, one may visit the first-floor rooms and see Dow's interpretation of First Period New England architecture, decorative arts, and domestic life. The Ward House restoration is notable as one of the first of its kind in the United States.

Since the City of Salem assumed ownership of the building in 1948, the Jonathan Corwin House, known more commonly as the "Witch House" (310½ Essex Street at North Street), has been maintained as a furnished historic site open to the public. Not surprisingly, over the last half century it has been a magnetic tourist attraction. Significant alone for its architecture, this symmetrical wood-frame and clapboard dwelling owes its notoriety to its association with the merchant Jonathan Corwin, who served as magistrate and justice during the Salem witch trials in 1692. Corwin had acquired the property in 1675 from Captain Nathaniel Davenport of Boston; the house was unfinished at that point. During the trials, many of those suspected of practicing witchcraft were brought to the house for pretrial questioning. One can only imagine these tense and dramatic personal confrontations. The house's popular name is hardly a misnomer and constantly inspires questions about its mysterious past.

In its restored form, the Corwin House belongs with

the Pickering and Ward houses as one of Salem's oldest and most significant early buildings. As completed, the house possessed a central chimney floor plan, a projecting two-story front central porch, flanking peaked gables, and a rear lean-to. On the front elevation, the entire second story overhung the first, with decorative drop pendants at the porch and end corners. At its center, the building was anchored by a plastered brick chimney. It remained in its original form until about 1746 when Sarah, the widow of Jonathan Corwin's grandson George, enlarged and substantially altered the appearance of the house to meet Georgian Colonial standards. Later owners made additional changes in 1856 and 1885, the latter resulting in a drugstore on the north end. When demolition threatened in 1945, Historic Salem, Inc., the local preservation group, bought the beleaguered property, facilitated its restoration, and passed it on to the city.

As a consequence of its association with Nathaniel Hawthorne and his celebrated novel *The House of the Seven Gables* (1851), the Turner House, or the House of the Seven Gables (54 Turner Street), is one of the nation's best-known historic sites and, like the "Witch House," a major visitor attraction. This much-reworked, rambling old mansion also merits recognition as an important example of seventeenth-century New England residential architecture. Built in 1668 for Captain John Turner, a prosperous merchant, the house was initially constructed on a two-and-one-half-story, two-room, central-chimney

> In the Turner House, history, literary tradition, and architecture combine to create an American icon.

plan, and it resembled the John Ward house, with two cross gables on the front facade. As his fortunes improved, Turner added a kitchen lean-to and the single-room-plan south wing with its own brick chimney and two-story porch. This new wing contained a second parlor, a chamber, and a garret with three gables, and it displayed an overhang with carved pendants and double casement windows. In 1692 John Turner, Jr., added a new north kitchen ell and installed the famous "secret staircase" in the rebuilt main chimney. In about 1725 he introduced additional stairs and Georgian-style details. Subsequent owners made further alterations.

In 1908, Caroline O. Emmerton, the founder of today's owning organization, The House of the Seven Gables Association, purchased the Turner House. She entrusted its restoration to Boston architect Joseph E. Chandler, an early practitioner of historic preservation. Although Hawthorne consistently denied that similarities existed between the Turner residence and the picturesque dwelling featured in *The House of the Seven Gables*, the book begins with a statement that irrefutably connects the two: "Half-way down a by-street of one of our New England towns stands a rusty wooden house, with seven acutely peaked gables, facing towards various points of the compass, and a huge clustered chimney in the midst. . . ." In the Turner House, history, literary tradition, and architecture combine to create an American icon.

The John Ward House, Brown Street. (Jim McAllister)

The Georgian Colonial Era, c. 1720–c. 1780

During the eighteenth century, as Salem began to prosper economically, extensive building activity occurred. With the exception of Newport, the city boasts the largest collection of Georgian Colonial residential architecture of New England's old seacoast communities. Sadly, most of Salem's high-style Georgian Colonial houses, principally on Essex and Washington streets, have been demolished. Surviving examples, distinguished by their gambrel roofs and rich, bold classical ornamentation, are the Lindall-Barnard-Andrews House (c. 1740), the Cabot-Endicott-Low House (c.1744–1748), and the Ropes Mansion (late 1720s). What survives in quantity from this era is a group of plain, vernacular dwellings, largely on Derby, Broad, and upper Essex streets. For the most part, they are modest, two-story, symmetrical, wood-frame and clapboard buildings, covered by pitched or gambrel roofs and displaying end or central chimneys as well as very basic pedimented or post-and-lintel doorway details.

Perhaps the finest example of this residential building type in Salem is the Crowninshield-Bentley House (126 Essex Street at Washington Square West). Today this historic house is open to the public and maintained by the Peabody Essex Museum. Built in about 1727–1730 for sea captain and fish merchant John Crowninshield, this chaste and nicely proportioned building is the epitome of a middle-class Georgian Colonial dwelling. Particularly notable is the perfectly symmetrical front elevation, with its reconstructed front central doorway flanked by flat Doric pilasters. Scholars believe that the house may have originated as a "half-house" (the east end) but was later enlarged in 1761 and 1794. In 1959–60, the structure was stripped of its more modern additions and moved to its present location from its original site behind the Hawthorne Hotel. The Essex Institute then restored it as a memorial to Louise DuPont Crowninshield, the highly regarded historic preservationist of Wilmington, Delaware, whose husband was related to the house's original owner.

Although four generations of Crowninshields lived in the house until 1832, it is primarily known for its association with the Reverend William Bentley, the minister of the First Church and an accomplished diarist, theologian, and history scholar. Bentley was a boarder here from 1791 to 1819, and while in residence he wrote substantial portions of his diaries, which are among the best sources on Salem life for this period. Around 1900, the Essex Institute published the diaries in edited form. Visitors to the house today may view furnished interior rooms that convey living conditions at the time of Bentley's residency.

Similar in form to the Crowninshield-Bentley House is the Derby House (168 Derby Street), on the grounds of the Salem National Maritime Historic Site. The oldest brick house in Salem, this striking two-and-one-half-story Georgian Colonial building was erected in 1761–62 by Captain Richard Derby for his son Elias Haskett Derby and Elias's new wife, Elizabeth Crowninshield. Over the next century other members of

> The Crowninshield-Bentley House is primarily known for its association with the Reverend William Bentley.

Crowninshield-Bentley House, 126 Essex Street. (Jim McAllister)

Derby House, 168 Derby Street. (Mark Sexton)

the city's leading merchant families (Nichols, Prince, and Ropes) owned and occupied the house. It then fell on hard times, but was rescued in 1927–28 by the Society for the Preservation of New England Antiquities, partially restored under the direction of George Francis Dow, and completed by the Park Service since 1938. Worthy of note is the superb brick detailing and the Tuscan Doric classical doorway with triangular pediment above. The kitchen ell was added in about 1790. Overlooking Salem Harbor, the Derby House, with its furnished, richly paneled interior rooms, constitutes a major part of the Park Service's riveting story of Salem's maritime heritage.

Samuel McIntire and the preeminence of the Federal Style, c. 1790–c.1830

Following the Revolutionary War, Salem experienced an era of maritime commercial prosperity unparalleled in its history. A principal outgrowth of the thriving local economy was a period of extraordinary architectural achievement. For three decades, from about 1790 to about 1830, the Federal style, derived from both English and American design sources, dominated the architecture of the city. All across the new nation, as well as abroad, Salem became recognized for its extensive and outstanding collection of Federal-style buildings. Primarily responsible for this legacy was Samuel McIntire (1757–1811), who became famed for his distinctive, personalized, delicate interpretation of the English Adamesque style. At the same time that McIntire was in active practice, other talented master builders and skilled artisans contributed to Salem's architectural heritage. Virtually synonymous with the Federal period, in Salem and throughout the United States, is the name of

Chestnut Street, regarded by many students of American history and architecture as one of the country's most noteworthy and magnificent residential districts. Its early-nineteenth-century character and appearance still largely intact, Chestnut Street preserves the work of McIntire and his contemporaries.

The most common type of Federal-style residential architecture present in Salem is the four-square, three-story mansion with low hip roof. Preserving the formal and elegant symmetry of the Georgian Colonial era, these aesthetically appealing buildings were constructed of brick as well as wood, with central hall plans and main center-front entranceways. Almost without exception, the principal visual focal point of this house type is a doorway featuring a semicircular or semielliptical fanlight above, with flanking rectangular sidelights. In many instances, the doorways are protected by rectangular or semicircular flat-roofed porticoes supported by columns and pilasters derived from ancient Greek and Roman models. Other common features include tall brick end chimneys, porch and roof balustrades, and narrow double-sash and Palladian windows. The finest of the city's early Federal examples, transitional buildings between the Georgian Colonial and Federal styles, are McIntire's Peirce-Nichols House (1782, 1801), the Joshua Ward House (c. 1784–1788), the Benjamin Hawkes House (1780; 1801), and the Joseph Felt House (1794–95).

The Peirce-Nichols House (80 Federal Street) merits closest attention. Long regarded as one of the most outstanding three-story wooden residences of its era in the United States, it displays tasteful elegance, lovely proportions, and bold classical details. Attributed to McIntire, it is believed to be his first major design com-

Peirce-Nichols House, 80 Federal Street. (Mark Sexton)

mission. Although the major portion of the house dates from about 1782, in 1801 McIntire remodeled several interior spaces, creatively combining his interpretation of the early Federal and later Adamesque Federal styles.

The Peirce-Nichols House, like so many other Salem mansions of its time, owes its existence to the profits of the booming international sea trade. The first owner was Jerathmiel Peirce, a leather dresser turned successful merchant, who with Aaron Waitt established the partnership of Peirce and Waitt, one of the country's most successful maritime trading firms. Peirce expended his profits generously to realize the house of his dreams. During the first phase of construction, the exterior was completed, along with the side stairs and most likely the rear stable with its pronounced arches. The primary exterior embellishment includes double roof balustrades, a round-arched rear window, monumental Doric corner pilasters, and front open and side enclosed Roman Doric porches with pediments and entablatures.

Upon the marriage of Sally Peirce to George Nichols in 1801, three interior rooms (hallway, east parlor, and chamber) were remodeled, making the house a superb document of changing cultural tastes and McIntire's architectural career. Also dating from this time are the one-story ell facing the stable court and the visually appealing front wooden fence with square posts topped by urns. In 1827, the property was acquired by George S. Johonnot but returned to the original owning family in 1840 when Jerathmiel's son-in-law, George Nichols, inherited it. The Essex Institute purchased the Peirce-Nichols House by subscription in 1917, but it was not opened to the public until the late 1930s. The Peabody Essex Museum administers the property today.

Dating from about 1800 to about 1815, the architecture of the mid–Federal period in Salem is lighter in feeling, less robust, and more refined than the city's early Federal buildings. Salem's most impressive and significant architecture dates from this era, which, not surprisingly, corresponds with McIntire's years of greatest productivity and accomplishment. In this brilliant building heritage, we may see not only the direct impact of McIntire, but also the indirect influence of Boston's Charles Bulfinch (1763–1844) and several other prominent New England designers and master builders. In Salem, the Adamesque Federal is most magnificently exhibited in structures such as McIntire's Assembly House (1782; c. 1797–98), the Gardner-Pingree House (1804–1805), the Clifford Crowninshield House (1804–1806), and the Cook-Oliver House (1802–1803; 1808); McIntire's Hamilton Hall (1805–1807); the Old Custom House (1805); the Old Town Hall and Market House (1816); and the Amos and Solomon Towne House (c. 1804), the White-Lord House (c. 1811), and the Dodge-Barstow-West House (c. 1802). Each of these buildings features subtly stated, attenuated, and beautifully executed classical elements, often highly geometric, with curved moldings, surfaces, and arches. Great flexibility and variation are evident in this ornamentation, as well as in the wall elevations and floor plans. The logic and elegance of this era in Salem architecture is approached by no other in the city's history.

Deserving of singular notice is the Gardner-Pingree

> Salem's most impressive and significant architecture dates from the mid-Federal period.

Gardner-Pingree House, 128 Essex Street. (Jim McAllister)

House (128 Essex Street), erected in 1804 and 1805 for the prosperous Salem merchant John Gardner, Jr. This magnificently proportioned and precisely detailed mansion is widely regarded as one of the most outstanding Adamesque Federal town houses in the United States and perhaps the premier example in New England. As a consequence, over the years it has been featured prominently in literature treating American architecture. Based on certain style features and documentary evidence, it has been traditionally attributed to Samuel McIntire and is considered by scholars to be the finest example of his most mature work. Some doubt about this attribution still exists, however, as early daybook entries make reference to several other local materials suppliers and artisans who were involved in the construction of the house. It remains difficult to argue, though, that the fine ornamentation of the exterior and the lavish wood carving and applied plaster decoration of the interior were not executed by McIntire. Among the building's most striking features are its beautifully balanced rectangular facade, a wooden roof balustrade, and, screening the front entrance, an elaborate semicircular portico with Corinthian columns and pilasters.

Adverse financial circumstances forced Gardner to sell his house in 1811 to Nathaniel West, who held title for just three years, selling it to Joseph White in about 1814. White's personal fortunes prospered as a result of the East India trade, which, unfortunately, led to his death by brutal murder in his bedchamber on August 6, 1830. Accused of this dastardly act were several local men, including relatives of White, who were seeking

> The logic and elegance of this era in Salem architecture is approached by no other in the city's history.

financial gain. Serving as prosecuting attorney in the widely publicized trial was Daniel Webster. After the trial, the house passed to Joseph's nephew Stephen, who sought a buyer for the ill-starred property. Finally, in 1834, it was sold to the first David Pingree, commencing almost a century of continuous Pingree family ownership. Heirs of the second David Pingree donated the house to the Essex Institute in 1933, and today, restored and fully furnished with high-style regional neoclassical furniture and decorative arts objects, it is open to public view under the administration of the Peabody Essex Museum.

Less recognized than the Gardner-Pingree House is McIntire's Cook-Oliver House (142 Federal Street), Salem's most notable and innovative Adamesque Federal wooden residence and also one of the masterpieces of early-nineteenth-century New England architecture. Designed by McIntire at the peak of his career, it was erected in 1802–1803 for Captain Samuel Cook. Records indicate that in 1808 McIntire further embellished the interior of the house. The rear ell was added about forty years later. After 1859, Cook's son-in-law, Henry K. Oliver, the former mayor of Lawrence and later mayor of Salem, lived here with his family. An amateur musicologist, Oliver composed the well-known and aptly titled hymn "Federal Street" during his residency.

Comprising three stories with a low hip roof, the Cook-Oliver House possesses a remarkable collection of delicate Federal-style elements, virtually all applied to the symmetrical front elevation. They include a modillioned cornice, molded window frames, a second-story horizontal belt course, and a central entrance with side-lights and a semi-elliptical fanlight above. Protecting this doorway is a graceful, flat-roofed porch displaying Doric columns and half columns, and beautifully carved embellishment. In front of the house is McIntire's finest surviving wooden fence, with urns and other decorative touches that resemble the treatment around the doorway.

Another mid-Federal-era building of note in Salem is Hamilton Hall (9 Chestnut Street at Cambridge Street), named in honor of Alexander Hamilton, the nation's first secretary of the treasury. This magnificent rectangular structure was erected between 1805 and 1807 at a cost of $22,000 as a social facility for the city's Federalist merchant families. The discovery of the first- and second-floor plans at the Essex Institute on 1954 validated the building as yet another Samuel McIntire commission. Long considered one of the most outstanding Federal-era public buildings in the United States, Hamilton Hall is noted for its refined but spectacular north side wall with McIntire-carved eagle and swags in panel inserts. The west gable end was largely completed in 1824, except for the doorway and Greek Revival portico, which was installed in 1845. In the past the first story accommodated caterers and shops; today, the upper two stories contain a ballroom, unusual for its "spring" dance floor, and a curved musicians' balcony. Hamilton Hall has remained a center of social and cultural activity for Boston's North Shore.

Although he died in 1811, McIntire's influence on Salem architecture lasted until the mid-1830s. During this period, the Adamesque Federal style reached its

> Although he died in 1811, Samuel McIntire's influence on Salem architecture lasted until the 1830s.

most advanced stage of development in the New Custom House (1818–1819, 1853–54), the Andrew-Safford House (1818–19), the Loring-Emmerton House (1818; 1885), the Forrester-Peabody House (1818–19), and the Dodge-Shreve House (1822–25). Less ornate Federal mansions such as the Pickman-Shreve-Little House (c. 1819) and the George Nichols House (1817–18) also continued to be built during this period, with the traditional square blockish form, hip roofs, tall end chimneys, and symmetrical front elevations. During the 1840s and 1850s, the brick commercial or housing row became popular in most American cities, and Salem was no exception. Excellent extant examples include the Bowker block (c. 1830), the Shepard block (c. 1850–51), and the Roberts-Shepard-Thorndike double house (c. 1830). Some transitional buildings, such as the Peabody Essex Museum's East India Marine Hall (1824–25), possessed Federal-style characteristics but also presaged the coming of the Greek Revival in both form and ornamentation.

Overlooking Derby Wharf and Salem Harbor next to the Derby House is the New Custom House (178 Derby Street at Orange Street), an imposing symbol of Salem's indelible presence in world maritime commerce and a superlative example of American Federal-style public building architecture. Import duties, an important source of revenue for the national government, were once collected here. The Custom House has a rich historical legacy, in large part because of Nathaniel Hawthorne's service here as surveyor of the port of Salem between 1846 and 1849. While he occupied this

Hamilton Hall, 9 Chestnut Street. (Mark Sexton)

post, Hawthorne collected material for what is arguably his greatest novel, *The Scarlet Letter,* the introduction of which contains a memorable description of the building, its occupants, and its important place in Salem's past.

Set on a high granite foundation, this elegant 1818–1819 brick edifice may be entered through a nicely articulated front central doorway screened by a balustraded porch that is supported by four attenuated Ionic composite columns. High on the roof balustrade, to use Hawthorne's words, is perched "an enormous (gilded) specimen of the American eagle, with outspread wings, a shield before her breast, . . . a bunch of intermingled thunderbolts and barbed arrows in each claw . . ." Dating from alterations made in 1845–46 and set atop the hip roof is an imposing Italianate cupola flanked by tall brick chimneys. Although the New Custom House was raised several years after McIntire's death, it resembles his older work, perhaps because four builders of his era—nephew Joseph McIntire, Jr., David Lord, Joseph Edwards, and Joseph True—are documented as having labored on the building. The Salem National Maritime Historic Site owns the building today and maintains a regular visitation schedule.

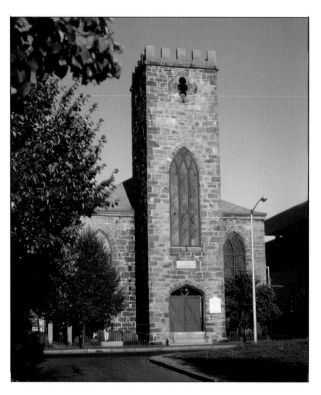

St. Peter's Church, 28 St. Peter Street.

Undeniably one of the most important examples of late Federal-era domestic architecture in New England is the Andrew-Safford House, situated on the west side of Salem Common (13 Washington Square West at Brown Street). This monumental neoclassical brick mansion was erected in 1818–19 for John Andrew, a local merchant who made his fortune in the Russian fur trade. It is Salem's most extravagant and flamboyantly detailed early-nineteenth-century dwelling and the city's consummate symbol of maritime success. The heaviness of its decoration anticipates the advent of the Greek and Italian revivals. One can only be impressed by the Corinthian-columned front entrance porch with balustrade, the elliptical-arched Palladian window above, the double roof balustrades, and particularly, the four freestanding three-story fluted columns on the south garden side. It has been conjectured that David Lord (1783–1845), the documented builder of the Dodge-Shreve House and one of the builders of the New Custom House, may have been the designer and contractor. After the Civil War, James O. Safford, a prominent Salem leather dealer, purchased the property, and it remained in his family until it was acquired by the Essex Institute in 1947. The Peabody Essex Museum owns the property today.

The near twin of the Andrew-Safford House is the Dodge-Shreve House (29 Chestnut Street), erected in 1822–25 for merchant Pickering Dodge by Lord and a crew of associates. Over the years, this well-proportioned, exceptionally lovely building has been owned by several prominent Salem families. In the first half of the twentieth century, when the Colonial Revival was popular in Salem, many of the house's exterior details were replicated in other local buildings, including several houses in the greater Chestnut Street neighborhood. Like the Andrew-Safford, the Dodge-Shreve House represents the last gasp of the fully developed Federal vernacular in the city. Among its most notable features are window lintels with Greek fret motifs, a balustraded Corinthian entrance porch, and a second-story modified Palladian window, identical to that of the Andrew-Safford House. The house is also noted for its interior marble mantels and a marble basement bathtub, supposedly Salem's first.

City Hall, 93 Washington Street. (Jim McAllister)

The Greek Revival and Victorian Eclectic styles, c. 1830–c. 1910

The eighty years between 1830 and 1910 in Salem saw a panoply of classical-derived and Victorian Eclectic architectural styles. Despite impressions to the contrary, the city's rich building heritage did not end with the Federal period. While design standards remained high, the pace of construction activity did slow down, as Salem made the transition from a predominantly maritime commercial to an industrial economy. Consequently, the earliest of the Romantic-era styles, the Greek Revival, had a less-powerful impact here than in other New England seacoast communities, producing only a few high-style examples. Fortunately, those that do exist are of outstanding architectural quality.

Salem may take great pride in its fine Greek temple–form granite buildings exemplified by the City Hall (1836–37) and the Old Essex County Courthouse (1839–41), both by Richard Bond (1797–1861), an accomplished Boston architect. Doubled in length in 1876, the City Hall (93 Washington Street) is distin-

Some of Salem's Architectural Treasures

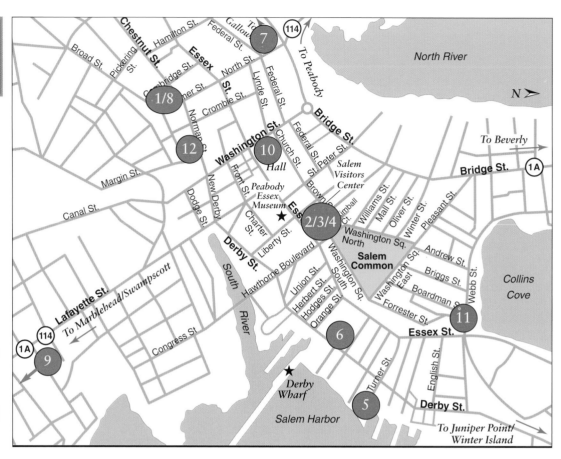

1. Pickering House (18 Broad Street). The oldest of the city's First Period residences, occupied by ten successive generations of Pickerings.

2. John Ward House (Brown Street) One of New England's finest seventeenth-century dwellings.

3. Crowninshield-Bentley House (126 Essex Street) Perhaps the city's finest example of Georgian Colonial architecture. Best known as the longtime residence of diarist Rev. William Bentley.

4. Gardner-Pingree House (128 Essex Street) Built for merchant John Gardner, Jr., and the site of the White murder.

5. Turner House (54 Turner Street) The home of Captain John Turner, known as "The House of the Seven Gables."

6. Derby House (168 Derby Street) The oldest brick house in Salem, built by Capt. Richard Derby as a wedding present for his son Elias Hasket Derby, who became the richest man in America.

7. Peirce-Nichols House (80 Federal Street) Believed to be the first design commission of architect and wood-carver Samuel McIntire.

8. Hamilton Hall (9 Chestnut Street) An important social and cultural facility since the early nineteenth century.

9. Henry Brooks House (260 Lafayette Street) One of Salem's only surviving Gothic Revival residences.

10. City Hall (93 Washington Street) Greek temple–form granite.

11. St. Nicholas Russian Orthodox Church (64 Forrester Street) Built in 1908 to serve skilled leather workers from Russia and Poland.

12. U.S. Post Office Building (Riley Plaza) This magnificent example of the Colonial Revival style recalls the work of Charles Bulfinch.

guished on its front elevation by four square Doric pilasters, seven beautifully articulated laurel wreaths in the entablature above, and, on the roof parapet, a gilded American eagle copied from one that Samuel McIntire carved for a wooden gateway formerly on Salem Common. Unquestionably one of New England's finest Greek Revival civic structures, the Old Essex County Courthouse (32 Federal Street) possesses twin gable ends, each with two tall Corinthian columns forming a portico framed by square Doric corner pilasters.

In many ways the antithesis of the Greek Revival, the early Gothic Revival also left its mark on only a few Salem buildings, but those that survive are superb. Two picturesque stone churches, St. Peter's (1833–34) and First (North) (1835–36), and one wooden residence, the Henry M. Brooks House (1851), are among the very best examples of this provocative style remaining in the country. St. Peter's Episcopal Church (28 St. Peter Street at Brown Street) is perhaps most characteristic of the ecclesiastical stone type, with its symmetrical plan; its wall and tower bat-

Henry Brooks House, 260 Lafayette Street.
(Jim McAllister)

tlements; its central, square, crenellated bell tower with wide, Tudor-arch doorway; and its large, pointed-arch windows with tracery and colored glass. Designed by the noted Boston architect Isaiah Rogers (1800–1869), St. Peter's was enlarged in 1845–46 with interior altar screen and window plans contributed by Richard Upjohn (1802–78), the renowned church architect from New York City.

An exquisite and dramatic building, the Henry Brooks House (260 Lafayette Street at Laurel Street) ranks as one of New England's most outstanding Gothic Revival residences and one of the gems of Salem architecture, there being no other examples of its style and type surviving in the city. It was erected in 1851 for Timothy Brooks, a local grocer, passing in 1854 to his son Henry M., who subsequently became president of the Forest River Lead Company, an active collector of historical artifacts, and a history scholar. Although the builder is unknown, the inspiration for the design was clearly a plan illustration from Andrew Jackson Downing's influential design book, *Cottage Residences* (1842). Contained in this perfectly symmetrical house are the same features present in the illustration—first-floor pointed-arch, leaded-glass windows; a steep-pitched front central gable with "ginger-bread" embellishment; an open porch with Tudor arches and miniature battlements; and rusticated flat wall boarding and corner quoins to simulate stone construction.

Almost a national style in the decade preceding the Civil War, the Italian Revival left its mark on Salem residential and public building architecture, both in stone and wood. One of the purest and best local examples is the John Tucker Daland House (132 Essex Street), today employed as a library and office facility by the Peabody Essex Museum. Erected as a residence in 1851–52 from plans drafted by Boston architect Gridley J. F. Bryant (1816–99), this imposing structure is one of New England's best surviving examples of the cube-type, one-family Italian Revival mansion. Prominent decorative details include a fine bracketed cornice, rusticated corner quoins and foundation stones, varied window treatments, and a ponderous rectangular front porch supported by paired Corinthian columns and topped by a

St. Nicholas Russian Orthodox Church, 66 Forrester Street. (Jim McAllister)

modified Palladian window, a vestige of the Federal era. Earlier roof balustrades and paneled chimneys, a Bryant trademark, were removed years ago. The house was constructed for Daland, another of Salem's prosperous merchants, and was occupied by his descendants until 1885 when the Essex Institute acquired it as its first permanent headquarters.

A wonderful late example of Victorian Eclectic architecture in Salem is St. Nicholas Russian Orthodox Church (64 Forrester Street at Webb Street), one of the finest Byzantine Revival ecclesiastical buildings extant in New England. Erected in 1908, it originally served a group of skilled leather workers from southern Russia and Poland who came to Essex County to work in the shoe and leather factories of Salem and Peabody. Architecturally, the building is distinguished by its five onion domes with patriarchal crosses and its front elevation with side towers and an ornate front-entrance porch canopy. It is a fitting capstone to a creative era in the development of the city's built environment.

John Tucker Daland House, 132 Essex Street. (Jim McAllister)

The Ascendancy of the Colonial Revival, c. 1889–c. 1940

Although Salem is primarily recognized for its stellar First Period and Federal-style architecture, the decades between the Civil War and World War II also produced some notable local buildings in a variety of vernaculars. Noteworthy are the many structures conceived in the Queen Anne, late Gothic Revival, Victorian Gothic, and Colonial Revival styles. This last style commands our foremost attention. Originating in Boston, the American Colonial Revival derives its principal elements from both the Georgian Colonial and Federal styles. Due in large part to the commanding presence of Samuel McIntire's work in Salem, the Colonial Revival made a deep impression locally, resulting in several excellent examples of this popular architectural idiom. Combining historical features with contemporary elements, buildings designed in this style emphasize classical correctness, strict symmetry, great scale, and rectangular floor plans, without distracting projections. Specific decorative details often include elaborate pilastered or columned doorways, semicircular and multistoried bays, roof balustrades and dormers, and Palladian windows.

The earliest local Colonial Revival buildings were constructed between 1889 and 1910 in the area of upper Essex and Chestnut streets. Reminiscent of the

Salem Athenaeum, 337 Essex Street.
(Jim McAllister)

Adamesque Federal are a group of houses erected in the district of Warren and Lafayette streets after the disastrous 1914 fire in Salem destroyed older buildings there. The third and most recent burst of construction took place from 1915 to 1940 and produced several outstanding public buildings around the city, as well as exterior and interior modifications to a number of Federal-era mansions. Of the public buildings, the Salem Athenaeum (1906–1907), the Masonic Temple (1915–16), the Lydia Pinkham Memorial (1922), the Hawthorne Hotel (Inn) (1924–25), and the U.S. Post Office Building (1932-33) merit special notice. The latter two structures were designed by Boston and Wenham architect Philip Horton Smith (1890–1960) of the firm of Smith and Walker. Nicely proportioned and handsomely adorned with Colonial Georgian and Adamesque Federal details, the Post Office (2 Margin Street at Riley Plaza) is without question Salem's most significant Colonial Revival civic edifice. It recalls the work of Bulfinch. This superlative collection of Colonial Revival buildings, culminating with the contributions of Smith, represents the last impressive phase of Salem's historic architecture and perpetuates the rich building tradition first displayed in the city's oldest seventeenth-century houses.

U.S. Post Office, Riley Plaza. (Jim McAllister)

The Turner House, or The House of the Seven Gables, where Hawthorne's portrait peeks through a window. (Mark Sexton)

Nathaniel Hawthorne: Salem Personified

He had just been decapitated. Playfully if somewhat lugubriously, that thought passed through the mind of Nathaniel Hawthorne as he stood at the top of the steps of the Salem Custom House, gripping the telegram from Washington. Ousted as surveyor of the revenue, he gazed through the masts of the ship *Eclipse* and the brig *Herald,* the only vessels docked at Derby Wharf.

"Not much left to survey anyway," he thought. "Mostly schooners with coal from Nova Scotia or wood from Bangor. The glory days of Surinam and Zanzibar are gone forever."

Under the circumstances, the *Eclipse* seemed an ironic emblem of the port's decades-long decline, and the *Herald,* of Hawthorne's own downfall. He was out of a job. He had expected this turn of events, but the news still stunned him. He lost sight of the harbor as he fell into a reverie, staring deep into the past. Perhaps he was thinking of late December 1807 when his father, captain of the brig *Nabby,* left this same port, never to return. Now he knew it was his turn.

It was a little after 6:00 P.M. The sun's oblique rays reflected the *Eclipse*'s rigging on the placid waters. Instinct kicked in. Hawthorne did what he had done countless times before at this time of the day. He took a walk. Today he would not go out to Juniper Point. At the foot of the steps, he strode slowly down Derby Street. As he passed Herbert Street, he studied his Manning grandparents' home, his mother's haven after his father died of yellow fever in Surinam. He had spent almost twenty-five years in that house. More than half the nearly hundred tales and sketches he had crafted had come to life in his chamber there under the eaves. Just ten years had passed since he had left the Manning home to become "a sort of Port-Admiral," as he jokingly referred to the job he took in 1839 as measurer of salt and coal at the Boston Custom House. It seemed like a lifetime ago.

He walked another block, turning right onto Union Street. He passed the house where he was born—his father's house—and came to Essex Street. With the sure foot of one who had made the trek many times, he turned left and began the walk up Salem's main thoroughfare, passing the cluster of banks in the city's commercial center. On the left, the East India Marine Society. His father had been elected a member the year Nathaniel was born. Next door stood the Essex Institute. He continued past the offices of the *Salem Register* and the *Salem Gazette,* glancing into Smith and Manning's livery stable before crossing Washington Street. As he passed the door of

Browne and Price Drugs, he looked for his friend Benjamin Browne. But the shop was closed for the day.

Ten minutes later, he reached the end of Essex Street and turned right onto Boston Street. The pungent odors of the tanneries shook him from his reverie just before he reached the home of tanner and currier Jacob Putnam, who stood in front of his door. With pipe in mouth, he cheerfully bid Hawthorne a good evening. Hawthorne looked away without reply, veered left past the house, and began the ascent of Gallows Hill.

"Queer fellow," muttered Putnam.

At the crevice near the top, he swung round to face east, casting his shadow and his eyes toward the port. But his mind was rooted to this spot, luxuriant with odious weeds. It had always made him feel uncomfortable. He remembered a phrase from one of his tales on witchcraft, "Alice Doane's Appeal" (1835), penned more than fifteen years earlier: "The dust of martyrs was beneath our feet."

He had been drawn to this site so many times by an unexplainable force, the same powerful compulsion he had portrayed in his fictional characters who were attracted to

Nathaniel Hawthorne's view of an empty Derby Wharf from the window of the Custom House.
(Mark Sexton)

the source of their pain. He had caught that feeling in the character of Reuben Bourne in the story "Roger Malvin's Burial" (1832). He had captured it again recently in the story of "Ethan Brand" (written prior to his dismissal and published in 1850). He felt it now, more sharply than ever. A succession of vague and fleeting impressions passed through his mind. He tried to call forth the image of his father captured in the miniature that his mother cherished. But all he could picture was a black-garbed figure, stern-visaged, bearded, sitting astride a horse and staring with an air of vindication at the corpse of a woman suspended from a rope.

"Father," he whispered urgently, in an effort to suppress the scene. That only summoned it more vividly. For an instant, he found himself in a state of drowsy consciousness between wakefulness and dreaming. Those dusk demons again. Shaking off the phantasm, he looked down the hill toward the intersection of Boston Street and the Salem Turnpike. Without much thought to obstacles in his path, he set out down the hill in a straight line for the corner, passing between the Hazelton and the Weston tanneries on his way.

Arriving at the intersection, he began to walk quickly down Essex Street. At Flint Street, he hesitated and then turned right. He had never done that before on his walks to Gallows Hill, but today an impulse prompted him to return to the town center by way of Chestnut Street. As he passed the long, stately brick mansion of the Saltonstalls, he thought again of his father, whose death at the age of thirty-three had crushed the Hathorne household's prospect of joining the families of other prominent Salem shipmasters and merchants on this fashionable street. Was it fate, fortune, or Providence? It didn't matter. He quickly passed the homes of the merchants Stephen Phillips and William Pickering. In a few moments, he arrived at the center of town. It was now 7:00 P.M. On his right, the day's last train for Boston was leaving the Eastern Railroad depot.

He crossed Washington Street diagonally and walked up Front Street to Charter Street, where he paused at the Old Burial Ground. Amidst the shadows of early evening, he could barely make out the headstone of Judge John Hathorne. His mind flashed back to the image he had imagined on Gallows Hill. He turned away and, reaching Newbury Street, began the final trudge past the stately elms of Washington Square, now confined behind the iron bars of a recently constructed fence, past East Church, and then down Mall Street, to the comforting arms of Sophia.

> Salem's intricate legacy of guilt and greatness, its dark persecutions and its brilliant voyages—and the great houses built on both—were, literally, in his blood.

Hawthorne's Salems

This scenario is fictional, of course. Call it a Hawthornean fantasy, if you will. But like Hawthorne's own fanciful tales, it aims at the truth and, in its essentials, is a faithful rendering of where Hawthorne stood, physically and emotionally, in June 1849 at about the time of his dismissal from his post at the Salem Custom House by the newly inaugurated Whig administration.

Salem's intricate legacy of guilt and greatness, its dark persecutions and its brilliant voyages—and the great houses built on both—were, literally, in his blood. Family history links him intimately to the subjects of the first three chapters of this book. These connections would influence his life and his career as an author. He was surely a son of Salem, the receptacle of its entire history, and a somewhat reluctant personification of it.

Almost forty-five years old, he was also out of a job. He had never been able to make a living as an author of tales. Less than two months later, his mother died. There was nothing left to hold him in Salem. Desperate for income to support his wife and two young children, Una and Julian (a third child, Rose, was born in 1851), he wrote furiously for the next nine months, producing his first book-length romance in more than twenty years. *The Scarlet Letter* (1850) would mark the beginning of a significant change of fortune for Hawthorne. Praised in all quarters as a masterpiece, the book would gain for him international recognition. But the book's introduction, called "The Custom-House," was also his parting shot at Salem. Within two months of the publication of the book, he left Salem for good, to return for only a few brief visits in the remaining fourteen years of his life.

No American author is as closely identified with a birthplace as Nathaniel Hawthorne. Yet his feeling for Salem was truly ambivalent. In fact, more of his writings are set in Boston than Salem. And though he resided in Salem for more than half his life, he only grudgingly acknowledged a certain amount of affection for the place while noting that he was "invariably happier elsewhere." The shabby town he describes in "The Custom-House"—with its plain wooden houses, its narrow lanes, and its unpicturesque main street—seems a world apart from the magnificent mansions on the west side of town that he shunned on his frequent walks to Gallows Hill. Hawthorne's Salem—Union Street, where he was born, and Herbert Street, where he spent much of his youth—was within earshot of the bustling docks and just a few blocks from the commercial center. It lacked, he felt, "the genial atmosphere which a literary man requires." Perhaps it was not a "genial" atmosphere. But the profound influence it exerted on virtually everything he wrote proves it an inspirational one. Toward his political enemies in Salem who had him fired, he expressed "infinite contempt." But he would never deny the predominant hold the town itself had upon his imagination.

Hawthorne's birthplace, 27 Hardy Street, formerly at 27 Union Street. (Jim McAllister)

Perhaps one should say "towns," for there was more than one Salem that inspired him. There was, of course, the Salem he was born into on July 4, 1804, still prospering from the daring maritime enterprise it had displayed for a generation in the East India trade. He was equally born to the Salem of earlier times, founded in 1626, one of the first English settlements in America. Hawthorne came to know them both intimately—the one, by walking its streets, the other, by reading its history. Though the biographical facts of his life are rooted in the boisterous commercial and political Salem of the nineteenth century, the psychological drama of his interior life and his writings draws its vitality from the more somber Salem of the seventeenth century and the seafaring Salem of the late eighteenth century.

Digging into his past

After his education at Bowdoin College, Hawthorne returned to Salem in 1825 to begin his preparation for a career as an author. Using his aunt Mary Manning's borrowing privileges at the Salem Athenaeum to immerse himself in local and regional history he also made a study of his paternal and maternal ancestry in New England. What he learned about Massachusetts Puritan culture both fascinated and repelled him. What he learned about his family patriarchs horrified him.

The political, social, and spiritual life of seventeenth-century New England colonists was dominated by a rigid Calvinist moral code emphasizing the sinfulness of humans. Enforcement of that code often sanctioned cruel and abusive punishment, including branding, dismemberment, and whipping. The less fortunate were hanged. Among the offenses: adherence to a dissenting faith. Among the offenders: a certain Quaker woman named Ann Coleman, ordered to be whipped through Salem's streets in the early 1660s by Major William Hathorne. Major Hathorne

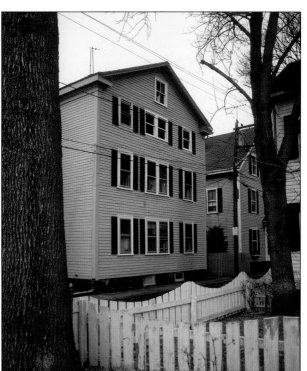

The Manning House, 12 Herbert Street, where Hawthorne wrote his early works. (Jim McAllister)

(Nathaniel added the *w* to the family name) established the family's patrimony when he arrived in Boston with the first wave of Puritan immigrants coming to the Massachusetts Bay Colony some thirty years earlier.

About thirty years after the Ann Coleman incident, Major Hathorne's son, Magistrate John Hathorne, presided at preliminary hearings of the infamous witch trials of Salem in 1692, pursuing evidence of guilt, by all accounts, with prejudice and with prosecutorial zeal. On his father's side of the family, therefore, Hawthorne discovered stern, bigoted, and superstitious Defenders of the Faith At Any Cost, including those who approved the humiliation, physical abuse, and execution of innocent women.

On his mother's side—the Manning side of the family—he found even more dirt. At about the same time Major Hathorne was railing against Quaker women, Nicholas Manning arrived from England and settled in Salem. Some years later, his wife accused him of incest with his two sisters. Nicholas fled to avoid prosecution. His two sisters were convicted and required to sit the next lecture day on high stools before the entire congregation in the Salem meetinghouse, with their crime written on paper placed upon their heads.

A more objective or callous observer might shrug off these dark family secrets as distant, irrelevant history or the fruits of individual character rather than family destiny. But Hawthorne could not do that. Studious, solitary, and introspective, a man of exquisite sensibility

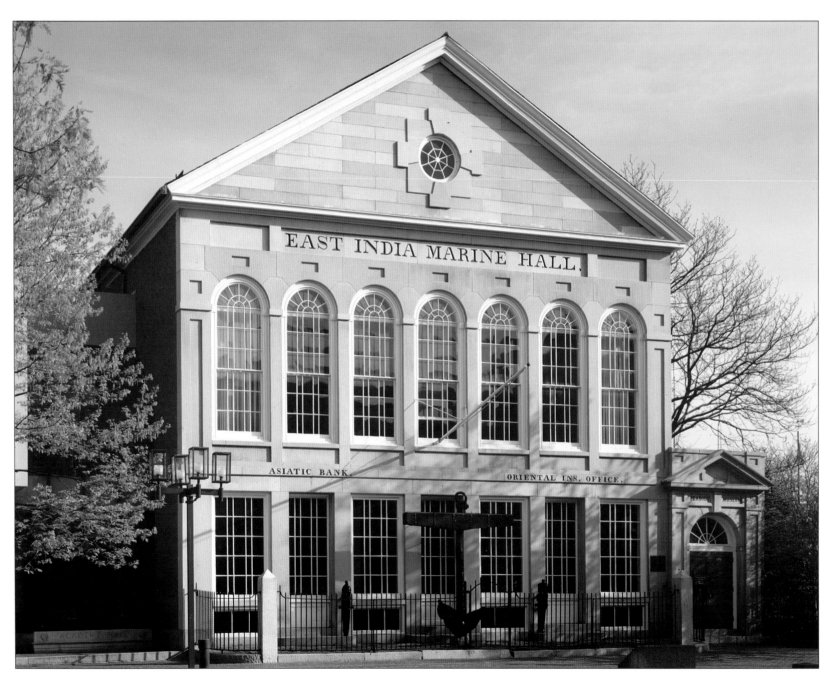

The East India Marine Society, now part of the Peabody Essex Museum. (Mark Sexton)

and melancholic temperament, Hawthorne both understood the full implications and felt the moral impact of his family's dark history. These incidents, he said, haunted him and gave him "a home-feeling with [Salem's] past" that he did not have toward the Salem of his time.

Perhaps this accounts for the dichotomy between the practical and fanciful sides of his nature. The practical side showed when he came home smeared with coal dust after a twelve-hour day of weighing coke as measurer of salt and coal at the Boston Custom House between 1839 and 1841. It emboldened him to milk cows, chop hay, and spread manure at the utopian community Brook Farm, where he resided for about six months in 1841. It prompted him to pull his boat out onto the Concord River on a summer eve in 1845 to help recover the body of a young woman who had committed suicide. It helped him efficiently perform his duties as corresponding secretary of the Salem Lyceum from 1848 to 1849. It made it possible for him to administer the estates of American seamen who had died under his jurisdiction when he served as American consul to Liverpool from 1853 to 1857.

The fanciful side prompted him to characterize himself as a "shadow" living amidst other shadows. In an 1840 letter to the woman he was then secretly engaged to, Sophia Peabody, he suggests that her love gave actual substance to his being that he otherwise would have lacked. He referred to his past experiences, including his decade-long period of seclusion and study at "Castle Dismal," as having the qualities of a dream. The preface

> No American author is as closely identified with a birthplace as Nathaniel Hawthorne. Yet his feeling for Salem was truly ambivalent.

to *The Blithedale Romance* (1852) describes his Brook Farm experience as a "day-dream." In "The Custom-House," written shortly after his dismissal from his duties as surveyor of the revenue, Hawthorne declares the whole experience a dream; his former coworkers are shadows, the merchants are only vaguely remembered, and Salem itself is "an overgrown village in a cloud-land." This ability to disconnect from "reality" is common in Hawthorne's fictional characters who embody many of his other attributes.

This does not suggest that Hawthorne was out of touch with reality. Far from it. His attention to the practical details of life was always in evidence. But his sense of reality was powerfully influenced by the magnet of a remote past. Although he had not actually lived in seventeenth-century Salem, he felt intimately connected to it. Maybe this is why he insisted upon "latitude" to move between the actual and the imaginary in the books he wrote in the 1850s, which he called "romances" rather than novels. It may have been easier to face the family skeletons in the transient and less tangible world of dreams.

Exorcising his past

In any event, the dark side of his family's origins reverberates in his fiction. The theme of incest finds its way into one of Hawthorne's earliest stories, "Alice Doane's Appeal." It is strongly hinted at in other works: his first romance, *Fanshawe* (1828); one of his best tales, "Rappaccini's Daughter" (1844); his last two completed romances, *The Blithedale Romance* and *The Marble*

Faun (1860); and some of the unfinished books he was working on at the time of his death in 1864.

Hawthorne alludes to the "grave, bearded, sable-cloaked" William Hathorne in the historical tale "The Gentle Boy" (1832), in which he sympathetically portrays persecuted Quakers in mid-seventeenth-century New England. The Quaker woman of this story, Catharine, has a rebellious nature, defies her persecutors, demonstrates profound love for her child, and eventually gains respect from the community that had earlier persecuted her. Readers of *The Scarlet Letter* will recognize in this woman with richly dark hair a model for Hester Prynne, whose challenge to Puritan Boston's righteousness and hypocrisy Hawthorne would unleash about twenty years later. Major Hathorne makes a cameo appearance in Hawthorne's best-known tale "Young Goodman Brown" (1835); in one of his history books for children, *Grandfather's Chair* (1840); and in his two most detailed accounts of early Salem history, "Main-street" (1849) and the Custom House sketch.

And then there is Judge John. More than either his Hathorne or his Manning predecessor, the witch trial magistrate looms over Hawthorne's life and writings like "the black mass of clouds" that sweeps over Goodman Brown's head as he rushes to a witches' sabbath. As Brown moves toward the view that all humans are evil, the voice of his wife, Faith, surely represents the innocent witch trial victims who preferred to die rather than profane their faith by admitting to guilt that they did not feel in their hearts.

In the hundreds of references to witchcraft in his fiction, Hawthorne was confronting family and communal history—a consistent, pervasive theme in his fiction from his first tale, "The Hollow of the Three Hills" (1830), published in the *Salem Gazette,* to the uncompleted manuscripts he was struggling with at the end of his life. The doubt, confusion, and conflict found in those last writings may reflect his poor ill health. But alchemy, witchcraft, and other diabolical forces intrude on these quests for nobility and immortality, suggesting that the demons of the past still haunted him.

Hawthorne did try to exorcise these demons. In "Main-street," a sketch of seventeenth-century Salem history, he expresses the somewhat anguished hope that the blood Ann Coleman shed when she was whipped on William Hathorne's warrant has been washed away with rains, "heaven's dew of mercy," that cleanse "the record of the persecutor's life."

In the sketch on Salem's Custom House, he confronts the powerful and mysterious hold that the town has on him. Still troubled by the possibility that the bloodstains of his ancestors' victims might yet linger unexpiated, Hawthorne takes these sins on his own shoulders and, in a remarkable acknowledgment of guilt, asks forgiveness: "I, as their representative, hereby take shame upon myself for their sakes, and pray that any curse incurred by them . . . may be now and henceforth removed."

Solemn as an oath, this ritual incantation was a plea to free his generation and his children's from the apparent curse that had haunted the family since the witchcraft trials. Maybe he viewed his forebears' sins as

> In the hundreds of references to witchcraft in his fiction, Hawthorne was confronting family and communal history.

Witch trials judge John Hathorne, an ancestor of Nathaniel Hawthorne, is among those laid to rest at the Burying Point on Charter Street. At right is the Peabody family home, where Nathaniel Hawthorne's wife, Sophia, lived before their marriage. (Jim McAllister)

Sophia Peabody Hawthorne, signed "JA" on the back and thus attributed to either Joseph Alexander Ames or J. Francis Alexander. (House of the Seven Gables)

Nathaniel Hawthorne by Charles Osgood, 1840. (Peabody Essex Museum)

Nathaniel Hawthorne's Salem

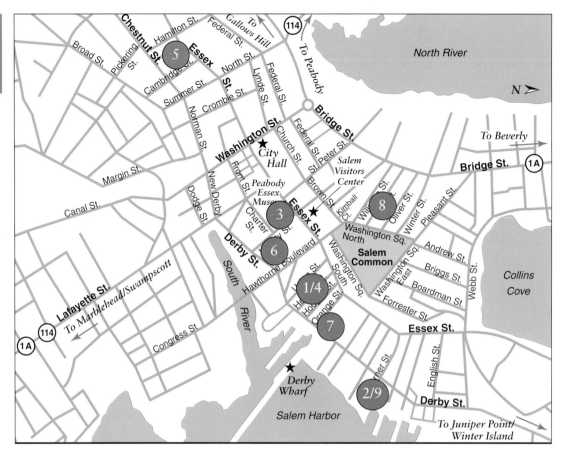

1. Original location of birthplace
Nathaniel Hawthorne was born July 4, 1804, in his father's house at 27 Union Street.

2. Current location of birthplace In 1958, the house in which Hawthorne was born was moved to 27 Hardy Street, adjacent to the House of the Seven Gables.

3. East India Marine Society Organized in 1799 and the cornerstone of today's Peabody Essex Museum. Hawthorne's father was admitted as a member in the year the author was born.

4. Manning Home (12 Herbert Street) The home of Hawthorne's mother's parents, where the author spent twenty-five of his years following his father's death at sea.

5. Salem Athenaeum Now at 337 Essex Street (site shown), this private library was in various locations during Hawthorne's lifetime. He used its collection to delve into Salem's and his own family's past.

6. Burying Point and Peabody Home
Side by side on Charter Street are two places with very different meanings for Hawthorne. Buried in Salem's oldest cemetery is his ancestor John Hathorne, a witch trials judge whose memory haunted him.

Next door at 53 Charter Street is the house where Hawthorne's beloved wife Sophia Peabody lived before they married.

7. The Custom House Built facing Derby Wharf in 1818–19, when Salem's "Golden Age" was already past, and now part of the Salem Maritime National Historic Site. Hawthorne's years here as surveyor of the port are the subject of his introduction to *The Scarlet Letter*.

8. 14 Mall Street In this house, Hawthorne wrote *The Scarlet Letter* during the year following his dismissal from the Custom House.

9. Turner House (House of the Seven Gables) Built for Captain John Turner in the seventeenth century and owned by Hawthorne's cousin Susan Ingersoll in the nineteenth, it suggested Hawthorne's romance *The House of the Seven Gables*.

responsible for "the dreary and unprosperous condition" of the Hawthorne family and the deeper cause of his own dismissal from the Custom House. His experience of false accusation (malfeasance in office), persecution by enemies, and execution (decapitation again) seemed to parallel the accusations, prosecutions, and executions of 1692. He portrays his dismissal as his share of the retribution for his family's past cruelty. Clearly, he wished to disengage himself from the curse, the family, and the town.

The House of the Seven Gables

It didn't work. He soon realized that he couldn't so easily throw off his past. Removed from political squabbling and the trauma of his mother's death, and buoyed by the critical success of *The Scarlet Letter,* Hawthorne drafted his most sustained examination of Salem during the fall and winter of 1850–51 in a remote cottage in western Massachusetts, where he and his family had moved in the late spring of 1850.

Once again, those grim grandsires of the seventeenth century loom large. In the preface to *The House of the Seven Gables* (1851), Hawthorne disavows any connection between the events of his "romance," as he insisted on calling it, and actual history. That disavowal may have been more fictitious than the story that followed. In *The House of the Seven Gables,* the fictional Judge Pyncheon is obsessed with uncovering the lost deed to a large tract of family land. In fact, descendants of William Hathorne spent the better part of a century in legal maneuvers intended to reclaim land in Maine acquired

> Hawthorne drafted his most sustained examination of Salem during the fall and winter of 1850–51 in a remote cottage in western Massachusetts.

by William but lost when the charter under which it was obtained was invalidated. In *The House of the Seven Gables,* the victim of a witch hunt, Matthew Maule, curses his accuser, Colonel Pyncheon (Judge Pyncheon's ancestor), with the words "God will give him blood to drink." Although the historical record indicates that Sarah Good uttered these words to the Reverend Nicholas Noyes just before her execution in July 1692, Hawthorne family tradition right up to Nathaniel's time maintained that they were spoken to Judge John Hathorne.

These echoes of seventeenth-century Hathorne family history sit side by side in the novel with portraits of characters drawn largely from attributes of nineteenth-century Hawthornes. The proud, refined, and aristocratic spinster, Hepzibah, mirrors the regal bearing and shabby gentility of Hawthorne's cousin Susan Ingersoll, owner of the house that today bears the name of the House of the Seven Gables. Hepzibah's reclusive habits, her dark dresses and melancholic disposition, reflect Hawthorne's memories of his widowed mother, Elizabeth. Phoebe's efficiency, grace, and sensitivity to her brother Clifford's moods, as well as her domestic competence, bespeak Hawthorne's wife, Sophia, whom he often called Phoebe. And Hawthorne wrote some of his own character traits into other characters. He certainly identified with Clifford's aesthetic detachment from the rude outside world. He even dressed Clifford in the faded damask purple dressing gown that he wore while writing *The House of the Seven Gables.* Holgrave, the slender, grave artist, like Hawthorne, views life from a distance and creates art revealing the real character of his subjects.

A sense of inevitable doom hangs over the house. It seems unavoidable that the sins of the fathers will be repeated by their descendants. Hawthorne is again squinting at those seventeenth-century Hathornes and Mannings. But his conclusion points in a different direction. Hawthorne asserts that the power of love can triumph over a curse set in motion by earlier generations. By the end of the work, the clouds have lifted, the villain is dead, and the good characters depart to the countryside, presumably to live happily ever after.

Hawthorne knew that life was rarely so rosy. At the time he was writing this novel, the Hawthornes were experimenting with country living. He soon became dismayed by the intemperate weather. ("I detest it! I detest it!! I detest it!!!" Hawthorne scrawled in his notebook. "I hate the Berkshires with my whole soul, and would joyfully see its mountains laid flat.") After only sixteen months, Hawthorne abandoned the pristine wilderness of Lenox and returned to the more congenial and cosmopolitan atmosphere of Boston and Concord.

Needlework sampler by Hawthorne's cousin Susan Ingersoll, 1777. (House of the Seven Gables)

But in the fictional world of *The House of the Seven Gables,* options were more limited. He could leave Phoebe and Holgrave in the house, subject to the malignant legacy of five generations of greed and treachery. His decision to spring them free, not merely a concession to public expectation of a happy ending, reveals his strong distrust of the notion of a house as a haven. Houses perhaps represented the insecuritites of life to Hawthorne. Changing houses was forced upon the family by his father's death and occurred at other critical junctures in his life. The first instance must have been deeply unsettling: abrupt removal from the house he was born in; adjustment to a new home full of grandparents, aunts, and uncles (ten people in all); the passive parental role and reclusive habits his mother developed in that house; the unwelcome role of his uncle Robert Manning as a surrogate father. Houses are abandoned in his early fiction on a whim ("Wakefield," 1835) or on an impulse ("Roger Malvin's Burial," 1832) and are crushed by a natural disaster ("The Ambitious Guest," 1835). These simple domiciles resemble the unpretentious Manning house on Herbert Street.

Hawthorne had few opportunities to view the interior of the more elegant dwellings of the town's wealthy merchant class. One came in 1838 during a brief flirtation with a Salem socialite, Mary Silsbee, whose father, like Hawthorne's, had been a sea captain. Unlike Captain Hathorne, Nathaniel Silsbee made a fortune on his voyages and lived a long life. In Hawthorne's fiction, mansions also have negative associations. In "The White Old Maid" (1835), an abandoned mansion becomes a kind of charnel house. In "Peter Goldthwaite's Treasure" (1838), the title character tears his mansion apart, board by board, looking for gold and silver. The once-stately mansion of royal governors in "Legends of the Province-House" (1838) has devolved into a tavern, its spacious chambers chopped up into cell-sized lodgings for near-indigent boarders. In "The Lily's Quest" (1839), a young couple build a magnificent mansion intended to be their "Temple of Happiness," which, when completed, becomes the tomb of the young woman.

Hawthorne was intimately acquainted with the Turner Street mansion, said to be the inspiration for the edifice in *The House of the Seven Gables*. As mentioned earlier, it was the property of Susan Ingersoll, a second cousin of Hawthorne's and about twenty years his senior. In the early 1830s Hawthorne enjoyed numerous pleasant evenings of playing cards and chatting about family history at the home of the woman he affectionately named "the Duchess." If the letter attributed to him by its recipient, Horace Conolly, Ingersoll's adopted son, is legitimate (the original is lost), Hawthorne toured the entire house in March of 1840 and learned on that occasion that it once had seven gables. It had only five then.

If the Turner Street mansion is truly the prototype for Hawthorne's fictional house, it has been substantially remodeled in the romance. No longer a cozy, comfortable center of social activity, it is transformed into the dark and decaying emblem of generations of human suffering—all occasioned by a seventeenth-century patriarch who accused someone of witchcraft. Sound familiar? Clifford describes the house to a passenger on a train as he and Hepzibah flee the domicile upon the death of Judge Pyncheon: "[T]hese heaps of bricks, and stones, consolidated with mortar, or hewn timber, fastened together with spike-nails, which men painfully contrive for their own torment" generate an "unwholesome atmosphere . . . rendered poisonous by one's defunct forefathers and relatives." They inherit, with the house, the worst attributes of their ancestors. To be rid of the sins, Clifford suggests that they must abandon the house.

Although Hawthorne largely depicted houses as repositories of past "sin and sorrow," one house revealed to him a future of hope: the Charter Street home of Sophia Peabody, which he first visited with his sisters in the late fall of 1837. Still a bachelor at age thirty-three, the reserved author found a soul mate in the equally retiring and soft-spoken young woman who would become the antidote to the melancholic mood that often shadowed him. They would not marry for close to five years, but in that intervening period, Hawthorne's "Phoebe" would attend to his deepest emotional and spiritual needs—buoying his spirits, chan-

> One house revealed to him a future of hope: the Charter Street home of Sophia Peabody.

neling his creative energy, awakening his powerful erotic instincts (the idealized Phoebe was also his "naughty Sophie"), and boosting his confidence through her nearly worshipful response to his fiction. Though she had been a lifelong invalid, Sophia's migraine headaches ceased with their marriage. The irresolute author of anonymously published tales and sketches now began his journey toward the full flowering of his remarkable talent.

In its houses and history, Salem gave Hawthorne the combustible material that fueled his mature fiction. In Sophia, Salem gave him the warm glow of a comforting home fire and unconditional support.

Hawthorne at sea

Hawthorne's future might have been radically different, and less secure, had he succeeded in obtaining a position as historian of a naval expedition to the South Seas under the command of Charles Wilkes. Had he received the appointment, he might have been too busy with preparations for the four-year circumnavigation to make the social call in November 1837 to the Peabody home, during which he met Sophia. The Wilkes expedition would have consumed the entire period that he instead spent in courting her.

On the expedition he would have followed in the footsteps of some of his forebears, including his father, by experiencing life at sea. The rigors and dangers of a long sea voyage would have opened to him another part of Salem's history—the southerly route followed by its shipmasters in their voyages to East Asia. A couple of years earlier, Hawthorne had begun to record his experiences in notebooks, and no doubt he would have continued this practice on such a momentous voyage of exploration. We can only speculate on what impact these notes might have had on his career as an author. Up to that point, the man from a family of seafarers, born within sight and sound of the port's thriving activities, had written little about the sea in his fiction.

According to his sister Elizabeth, some stories in a projected collection written in the late 1820s, *Tales of My Native Land,* focused on the sea. In a fit of frustration, Hawthorne burned them. After that, the sea appears incidentally in a few works, usually with a hint of disaster in the background. In "The Wives of the Dead" (1831), one of the principal characters is the widow of a sailor. In "Chippings with a Chisel" (1838), a woman visits a tombstone carver to have a monument built for her first love, killed by a whale in the Pacific forty years earlier. In "Footprints on the Sea-shore" (1838), a beachcomber ruminates on sunken ships and corpses. The cheerful reflections of an aging fisherman in "The Village Uncle" (1835) strike a somewhat more positive note. But even he seems intent upon coloring the past in order to compensate for the debilities of old age.

It also seems odd that some of Hawthorne's most significant friendships did not inspire literary ventures into a subject so central to the history of his family and native town. Horatio Bridge, a classmate at Bowdoin and a lifelong friend, was an American naval officer whose manuscript on his experiences at sea, *Journal of an African Cruise* (1845), Hawthorne revised and edited

> Hawthorne's future might have been radically different had he succeeded in obtaining a position as historian of a naval expedition to the South Seas.

for publication. Another college friend, Henry Wadsworth Longfellow, who, like Hawthorne, grew up in a busy seaport (Portland, Maine), must have often talked to him during their numerous dinner engagements about the sea subjects he used in his poetry. Also, Herman Melville, a neighbor whose friendship Hawthorne valued during his residence in Lenox, must have entertained him with accounts of his whaling and naval adventures.

His nonliterary sources of employment (the Custom House job in Boston, his surveyorship at the Salem Custom House, and his position as consul to Liverpool) put Hawthorne in direct daily contact with virtually every activity and challenge of the maritime world, including the countless yarns he must have heard from boastful young sailors and nostalgic old salts. A handful of these were recorded in his notebooks, but none were to appear in his fiction. This facet of Salem's and his family's past did not resonate in him as the subject of witchcraft did. Despite his preference for seaside residence, his fondness for sea voyaging, and his belief in the bracing and therapeutic influences of coastal living, he studiously avoided the subject in his fiction.

In 1852, Herman Melville sent Hawthorne a letter

The Hawthorne children, Una, Julian, and Rose, 1860. (Peabody Essex Museum)

with details of a story he had heard while visiting Nantucket, of a woman named Agatha. Her sailor husband had abandoned her two years after they were married, but returned seventeen years later with an offer of financial help. He did not tell her that he had remarried. Melville urged Hawthorne to work this sketch into a romance. He never did, but in a sense he already had.

As *The Scarlet Letter* opens, Hester is released from jail and takes up residence with her infant daughter, Pearl, in a cottage by the sea, isolated from the community that has ostracized her. There they live for the next seven years, the child fatherless, the woman a virtual widow. In the ensuing pages, the child searches for her father and the woman is betrayed by her husband and abandoned by her lover, in many ways reflecting the Agatha story well before Hawthorne had heard it from Melville. In Hawthorne's story, Pearl eventually moves across the sea to a domestic life of security, prosperity, and happiness. For Hester—her cottage now adorned with tokens of Pearl's loving remembrance of her—the sphere of her sin and sorrow becomes the province of her life's work to comfort and counsel others. Perhaps this was Hawthorne's romance of the sea.

Another stroll through Salem

Nathaniel Hawthorne stepped slowly out of the shadows of his Mall Street home in the early afternoon on the day after his "decapitation." He blinked in the strong sunlight and thought momentarily of retreating, but trudged on. He had a book on the War of 1812 in his left hand, which he had borrowed from the Salem Athenaeum a couple of days earlier but no longer cared to read. He would return it, buy a cigar, and then, who knows? He was restless.

He made his way to Essex Street. John Chapman, editor of the *Salem Register,* stood by the door of his office, giving instructions to a messenger. Hawthorne passed him without a word or a glance.

Whig-wag! Slang-whanger! What venom have you prepared for me today? Hawthorne was surprised by the vehemence of his own thoughts. A moment later, he found himself standing in the office of the *Salem Gazette.* Caleb Foote, the editor, looked up from his desk in agitation.

"I come for news of the day, Caleb," Hawthorne said.

Bela Lyon Pratt statue of Nathaniel Hawthorne on Hawthorne Boulevard. (Jim McAllister)

"It's not all good news, is it, my dear man?" Foote replied. "I am sorry, Nat. I did not push for this, you know."

"Be at ease, Caleb," replied Hawthorne, sensing Foote's embarrassment. "I have come to understand the modes of political action too well to be distressed by my, shall we say, execution. We know how the world works. You have your business. As for me, this job has paid the bills but it has been a bore and a thralldom. The chains are off. I am . . ." He hesitated for a moment. "I am free."

"You leave Salem?"

"As soon as I have the means," replied Hawthorne. His gray eyes narrowed. "And pay off a few debts," he added.

He picked up a copy of the day's newspaper and backed out of the door, repeating as he left, "Be at ease, Caleb."

At the door, he glanced in the direction of the Athenaeum but retraced his steps toward the town's wharves. He paused at Newbury Street and opened the newspaper. At the bottom of page two, he found what he was looking for: "Allen Putnam, of this city, has been appointed Surveyor in room of Nathaniel Hawthorne, removed."

"Very clean, almost bloodless," he thought.

He continued to walk, with a stronger gait now, down Essex Street. As he reached the rear of the Custom House, he heard the creak of pulleys and the shouts of dockworkers on Derby Wharf. The barque *Lewis* had been cleared the day before for Zanzibar. "Perhaps it will sail today. Perhaps not. No matter. I am done with all of that," he asserted.

At Turner Street, he turned right and made his way down to Derby Street, pausing at the intersection to gaze in the direction of the harbor and the Duchess's house. Even in the sunlight, its brown timbers, weather-worn by nearly two centuries of east winds, assumed a rusty appearance, as if forged in iron.

"What history there," he mused. "What secrets." As he stared at the house, he was struck by the thought that he was gazing at the chronicle of Salem's entire history, and his own.

"By and by, I will make something of that," he reflected, as he turned eastward up Derby Street. A short time later, he passed the ropewalk on his left at Collins Cove and then the almshouse. He looked to his right and noticed cousin Ebenezer Hathorne's old farmhouse precariously perched at the top of Hollingsworth Hill at Hathorne's Point. He was heading for Juniper Point.

When he arrived, he looked out to the open sea. He remembered the one word he had whispered the day before at the top of Gallows Hill. He wondered how his father would have faced this crisis. He had been told that his father was a strong, stern, and silent man, not given much to fussing over life's haphazard turns of chance. He thought of his aging mother, now sixty-nine years old and in failing health. Despite her infirmities, she remained in his mind the picture of reserved and quiet refinement and dignity. He summoned up an image of the children, Una and Julian, recovering from scarlet fever but flushed with the roseate beauty of their budding lives. And then he remembered Sophia. She had taken the news like a woman—that is, better than a man. She was tending to the needs of the children. She would take care of his mother. She was his rock.

He looked back toward the pastures and the mowing fields on the slope behind him. He was struck by the beauty of a moss-covered willow tree, shimmering and glowing in a concert of sun and wind. Above, three herring gulls swayed and floated, as if in a trance induced by the air's narcotic scent. A milkweed butterfly hovered near a cluster of beach roses for a moment, its delicate golden and black wings radiant in the sunlight, and then made its way inland. He followed it with his eyes until he could see it no more.

He turned back to the sea. He was focused now, calm, deliberate, and, for the moment at least, at peace. He stared out into that wilderness of water and, for the first time in his life, he felt free.

> As he stared at the house, he was struck by the thought that he was gazing at the chronicle of Salem's entire history, and his own.

Plummer Hall, built for the Salem Athenaeum, now houses the Phillips Library of the Peabody Essex Museum. (Jim McAllister)

Salem Then and Now

Salem at the time of Nathaniel Hawthorne's death in 1864 bore little resemblance to the bustling seaport of his youth. The color and excitement of the East India trade had been replaced by the plain, steady hum of modern industry. Salem would grow and experience great change for the next half century. And during that time, its citizens were too busy coping with change and building their future to think much about Salem's remarkable maritime and architectural heritage, its infamous witch trials, or even the famous, but locally unpopular, Nathaniel Hawthorne.

Salem had been incorporated as a city in 1836 and had adopted a new form of government that featured a mayor, a common council, and a board of aldermen. A city seal and motto, "To the farthest ports of the rich east," had been adopted and a new city hall had been built on Washington Street with federal money. The population had swelled from 9,457 in 1800 to over 22,000 in 1864, and it would double again by the time of the great Salem fire of 1914. Many of Salem's newer citizens had fled the famine in Ireland.

The city had blossomed as a cultural center during Hawthorne's lifetime. Residents and visitors could now visit the famed East India Marine Hall (built in 1824–25) on Essex Street, where they could view artifacts and curiosities gathered from the far corners of the earth by seafaring members of the Marine Society. Intermingled with ship models and paintings were nose flutes, war clubs, and even a shrunken head from the tiny islands of the East Indies.

Almost opposite the museum stood Plummer Hall (1856–57), the Salem Athenaeum's new home. The Athenaeum was organized in 1810 when the Social Library and Philosophical Library merged, and it possessed the world-renowned Kirwan Scientific Library captured by a Beverly privateer during the Revolution. Nathaniel Bowditch (1773–1838), Salem's great navigator and mathematician, made good use of the Kirwan collection, just as Hawthorne had devoured the Athenaeum's biographies, histories, romances, and a sampling of just about everything else.

The first floor of Plummer Hall was leased to the Essex Institute, which had also been formed by a merger. The Essex Historical Society and Essex County Natural History Society had joined forces in 1848 and were collecting publications, historical objects, and natural artifacts primarily relating to Essex County. Early in the twentieth century the institute would take the lead in the Salem preservation movement.

Two other important Salem cultural institutions were the Salem Charitable Mechanics Association (1817), which sponsored Thursday evening lectures related to science and industry, and the Salem Lyceum Society. The Lyceum was organized in 1830 and built a hall on Church Street the following year. At the time of Hawthorne's death, the society was at the midpoint of a sixty-year, one-thousand-lecture run. John Quincy Adams, Daniel Webster, and Henry David Thoreau were just a few of the brilliant nineteenth-century intellectuals who appeared on the Lyceum stage. Hawthorne was one who didn't, but he did serve as corresponding secretary for the Society in 1848–49.

On February 12, 1877, Alexander Graham Bell would appear at the Lyceum to demonstrate for the public, for the very first time, a new invention called the telephone. The conversation between Bell and his partner, the Salem native Thomas Watson who spoke to him from Boston, could be heard clearly by all in attendance. A patent for the telephone had been awarded the previous year to "Alexander Graham Bell of Salem, Massachusetts." Bell lived on Essex Street from 1873 to 1876.

Salem residents could choose from a broad spectrum

Elizabeth Palmer Peabody.
(Peabody Essex Museum)

of cultural pursuits, including performances by music societies, chorales, and theatrical groups. The three-hundred-member Salem Oratorio Society and the famed Salem Cadet Band would be organized after the Civil War. A driving force behind the Salem music scene was Henry Kemble Oliver of Federal Street. A military leader, businessman, and statesman who served as mayor of both Salem and Lawrence and as state treasurer of Massachusetts, Oliver also composed music, played at least a half dozen instruments, and was said to have the "sweetest voice in Essex County" even in his seventies.

This cultural environment nourished writers, educators, and artists in significant numbers. Hawthorne's sister-in-law, Elizabeth Palmer Peabody (1804–1894), founded the American kindergarten movement with help from her sister Mary (1806–1887), the wife of educator Horace Mann. Elizabeth was also a charter member of the Transcendentalist Club, which gathered in her Boston bookstore and included Ralph Waldo Emerson, Bronson Alcott, and William Ellery Channing. Peabody championed the writers Hawthorne and Jones Very (1813–1880), Salem's renowned Transcendental poet. Very, a Harvard tutor turned minister and a brilliant Greek scholar, composed intensely mystical poems.

William Wetmore Story (1819–1895), the son of associate U.S. Supreme Court justice Joseph Story, was born and raised in his father's Washington Square mansion. William abandoned a successful career in law to pursue the arts of sculpture and poetry. He moved to Rome, where he built a reputation as one of the most important American sculptors of his time. Hawthorne helped immortalize Story's statue *Cleopatra* by featuring it in his romance *The Marble Faun*. A half century later, another Salem artist, Frank Weston Benson, would be called "the nation's most medaled painter" by a Boston newspaper. Benson's impressionistic portraits and etchings of outdoor hunting and fishing scenes hang in many major U.S. museums.

Salem also now had its own college. The Salem Normal School opened on the corner of Broad and Summer streets in 1854 and offered training for prospective teachers. The Normal School would move to south Salem at the end of the century and, as Salem State College, would become a major force in regional education and culture.

Just two years after it opened, the Normal School admitted its first African-American student. Charlotte Forten moved to Salem from Philadelphia and matriculated at the school in 1856. A few years after graduation she moved south where she would have a successful career as a teacher, poet, and essayist.

While attending the Normal School, Forten lived with the family of Charles Remond. Charles and his sister Sarah were raised in Salem and went on to become important African-American figures in the abolitionist movement. Both traveled extensively in the United States and the British Isles, lecturing on the evils of slavery. Sarah eventually settled in Italy and became a physician.

Sarah Parker Remond. (Peabody Essex Museum)

Salem's African-American community had its own school and church. The latter opened in 1828 and was just one of a number of churches to appear in the city during Hawthorne's lifetime. Between 1804 and 1864, Salem's Congregational and Anglican churches were joined by others organized by Baptists, Methodists, Catholics, and Universalists. A Mormon church opened in 1842, but closed two years later after many of its one hundred members moved on to Nauvoo, Illinois. The Second Advent Church (1845), whose congregation was waiting for the world to end, was a fixture in Salem longer than expected. Other houses of worship would appear later in the nineteenth century.

New industry

The most dramatic change in Salem during Hawthorne's lifetime was the demise of the city's East India trade and the emergence of new industries. The earliest and most important to develop was the leather business. Tanneries had been present in Salem since 1639, when Philemon Dickinson opened a tanning operation on the eastern side of present-day Salem Common. Maps of that area show three sizable tanneries in operation in about 1780. But within a decade the move to Blubber Hollow had begun.

Vestige of the days when Blubber Hollow was Salem's leather district. (Jim McAllister)

Blubber Hollow sits at the base of Gallows Hill and at one time was bisected by the North River. The area may have derived its name from the whale blubber from which tanning oils were once extracted. Hides for tanning were imported from areas as close as Gallows Hill and as far as Africa and South America. Tough African hides, piled on the river bank to be softened by the salt water and sun, were a common sight.

Many early tanneries were built on the slopes of Gallows Hill itself, and a number of streets in that area, including Varney, Putnam, Nichols, and Pope, bear the names of their owners. By midcentury, more than eighty tanning or currying shops were operating in the hollow and along both sides of the North River, employing 550 workers. By 1885, that number would nearly double.

Many of the workers were Irish immigrants, and soon the Boston Street neighborhood was crammed with new rooming houses, apartments, and small starter homes built to meet their housing needs. Eventually a number of the Irish leather workers opened their own shops.

The tannery owners were a close-knit group and gathered regularly at the supply house of Joshua Grant. Known as "The Senate," they exerted much power in the leather industry. In July 1886 they squared off against their workers in a strike called by the Knights of Labor. The workers protested long hours, low wages, and, most importantly, the unwillingness of the owners to negotiate with a union. The strike lasted five months and was marked by many acts of violence against the non-union workers brought in by the tannery owners. One of the strike leaders, George Warren, was found with a bullet in his head, and the workers who joined the Knights of Labor were excommunicated by the Catholic Archdiocese of Boston. Eventually the striking workers became tired of the violence, and at the end of November they returned to work.

The strike was the first blow to the city's leather industry. By the 1920s most of the large shops had closed, victims of labor problems, competition from the growing leather industry in the Midwest, the scarcity of bark mulch needed for tanning, and the Salem fire of 1914.

Prior to the Civil War, the Salem tanneries primarily produced leather for work shoes worn by slaves on Southern plantations. Thus it was natural that shoe factories would also locate in Salem. Both tanning and shoe industries suffered difficult times early in the Civil War when their major market suddenly disappeared. But many local factory owners were saved by the Union army, which ordered shoes for the troops. By the time of the leather strike in 1886, nearly 850 people were employed in various aspects of shoe production.

The largest Salem shoe factories were situated near the leather shops in Blubber Hollow, but the real center of the Salem shoe industry was in downtown Salem between Washington and Lafayette streets, in close prox-

The Salem depot of the Boston and Maine Railroad, about 1897.
(From Illustrated History of Salem and Environs)

imity to the Eastern Railroad train depot. The train was routed through Salem from Boston in 1838 and helped fuel the city's industrial expansion.

The Eastern Railroad (later the Boston and Maine) was not the only train through town. In 1850, the Salem and Lowell Railroad, under president Stephen C. Phillips, began transporting coal and cotton from Phillips's wharf at the head of India Street to the textile mills in Lawrence and Lowell. Transshipment of coal would remain a vital Salem industry well into the twentieth century. Phillips Wharf would later be leased and operated by the Boston and Lowell Railroad for the same purpose. The property was incorporated into the New England Power Company complex in the late 1940s.

By 1847, the citizens of Salem had built their own cotton mill on Stage Point and could boast that it was one of the largest in America and one of the first to be powered by steam. Nathaniel Griffin, a former sea captain, had convinced nearly fifteen hundred residents of the area to buy stock in the Naumkeag Steam Cotton Company, which commenced production of cotton

Not even the fire station on Lafayette Street (top left) was saved in the Salem fire of 1914. St. Joseph's Church (right) and hundreds of other buildings were destroyed, leaving thousands without homes and many camping out on the Common. (Postcards courtesy of Jim McAllister)

sheeting in 1847. Coal and lumber supplies were stored on Union (now Pickering) Wharf. The wharf and mills were connected by a bridge built across the South River. The Naumkeag Mills soon became nationally known for the Pequot brand of sheeting, and the company eventually employed over two thousand people.

French Canadians poured into Salem to work in the mills and settled in the nearby neighborhood, which came to be known as "La Pointe." The mills also provided employment for other immigrant laborers, including Russians, Poles, and Italians, who settled in Salem in large numbers in the late nineteenth and early twentieth centuries.

The fire of 1914

Much to the horror of the employees and the rest of the local populace, the Naumkeag Mills were completely destroyed in the Salem fire of 1914. The blaze began with an explosion on June 25 in the Korn Leather Company in Blubber Hollow. Over the next thirteen hours it worked its way eastward toward the waterfront. Fire companies from as far away as Hingham responded,

The maker of Monopoly was a leading employer beginning in the late nineteenth century. (Jim McAllister)

but some had to stand by helplessly because their equipment couldn't be connected to Salem's Lowry hydrants. The blaze destroyed eighteen hundred buildings, including forty-one factories. More than five thousand people were suddenly out of work, and thirty-five hundred families found themselves homeless. Some of the latter spent the summer in a camp in Forest River Park.

Immediately after the fire, the directors of Naumkeag Mills voted to rebuild the plant. The company continued operating at Stage Point until it moved to South Carolina in 1953. The property was later developed as a waterfront industrial and office park.

Some of the other industrial concerns operating in Salem in the latter part of the nineteenth century produced chemicals, white lead, paint, typewriters, and jute bags. They were joined by the Salem Gas Light Company (1850), the Salem Electric Lighting Company (1882), and Parker Brothers Game Company (1883). Parker Brothers was started by George Parker, a sixteen-year-old Salem High School student and board game aficionado. When George invented and published with his own money a card game called Banking, school officials gave him time off from

A view of the Naumkeag Mills complex, now Shetland Properties, from the House of the Seven Gables. (Jim McAllister)

his studies to make sales calls. The venture was a success, and a few years after graduation George built a factory on Bridge Street. He eventually brought his brothers Charles and Edward into the business.

Many of the company's early games, including Tiddledy Winks, Battle of Manila, and Klondike, were related to current events or fads. The three card games Rook, Pit, and Flinch were early Parker Brothers hits, as was Ping-Pong, the table tennis game. The American rights to the latter were obtained from a British firm in 1902 and held by Parker Brothers until 1971, when they were sold to the Harvard Table Tennis Corporation. The Salem company's most successful game, Monopoly, was at first rejected as having "52 fundamental playing errors." Fortunately, Parker reconsidered and came to own one of the the best-selling board games ever produced. Parker Brothers was a family-owned business until 1968 when it was sold to General Mills. The manufacturing operation was moved out of Salem in 1991.

Another well-known company with Salem roots is Sylvania. The Hygrade Incandescent Lamp Company moved into Blubber Hollow soon after the Salem fire in 1914 and later, in 1931, merged with a company from Pennsylvania named Nilco Lamp–Sylvania Products. The new company made incandescent light bulbs and radio tubes and became a world leader in those industries. Sylvania was a presence in Salem until the 1990s.

The Russian Aid Society was one of many organizations that helped Salem immigrants adapt to their new home. (Jim McAllister)

Newcomers to Salem

The continuing influx of immigrants into Salem meant plenty of new customers for the city's retailers. And the Salem downtown shopping district, centered at the intersection of Washington and Essex streets, would grow by leaps and bounds in the last quarter of the nineteenth century as Salem's trolley system continued to expand. The first horse-drawn trolleys began transporting passengers from the city's outlying neighborhoods in 1862, and over the next few years extended their routes to neighboring communities. By the time the trolleys went electric in the early 1890s, the city's retail volume had doubled, and Salem was on its way to becoming one of New England's busiest shopping centers. Eventually one could shop at Sears and Roebuck, Kresge, F. T. Woolworth, W. T. Grant, Almy's, Webber's, and Empire department stores—all within three blocks on Essex

Street. The downtown would be a legitimate boomtown until the North Shore Shopping Center opened on Route 128 in Peabody in 1958.

The expanding immigrant population also brought social problems. In the latter part of the nineteenth century, issues related to housing, crime, medical care, and unemployment needed to be addressed. Public meetings sponsored by groups such as the Women's Moral Society and private gatherings of the city's leading citizens led to the formation of the Woman's Friend Society, the Plummer Farm School, a half dozen temperance societies, and other organizations designed to address Salem's social ills.

No one did more to ease the city's social pressures than the Bertram and Emmerton families. John Bertram amassed a fortune in the maritime trade and railroads, and he plowed much of it back into the Salem community. Bertram organized and helped fund the Salem Hospital and the Bertram Home for Aged Men. After his death, his family gave the captain's mansion to the city for its public library. Bertram's granddaughter, Caroline Emmerton, organized and funded baby-weighing stations, to provide medical care for immigrants, as well as the Public Welfare Society, which served as a clearinghouse for the sometimes disorganized Salem social service delivery system. "Miss Emmerton" was also a major supporter of the Salem Fraternity Boys' Club and the driving force behind the founding of the House of Seven Gables Settlement House, a multifaceted service center for immigrants, in 1907.

The following year, in a move that would provide future financial stability for the settlement house, Caroline Emmerton bought and restored the Turner-Ingersoll House. In 1910, the house, now known as the House of the Seven Gables, was opened as an income-generating museum. The restoration of this seventeenth-century waterfront mansion was a defining moment in the renewal of public interest in Nathaniel Hawthorne and colonial architecture, two of Salem's "cornerstones," and the development of Salem's future tourism industry.

> No one did more to ease the city's social pressures than the Bertram and Emmerton families.

Preservation begins

One of the primary problems the city faced in the half century after Hawthorne's death was the lack of housing for its growing immigrant population. The solution in many cases was to subdivide existing homes or to raze them and build large multifamily tenement houses. Unfortunately, little thought was given to the possible architectural significance of these older structures, and many seventeenth- and eighteenth-century buildings disappeared from the Salem landscape. When Caroline Emmerton bought the Turner House and hired preservationist Joseph Chandler to oversee its restoration, she was taking the first step to reverse that trend. The Salem preservation movement was underway.

The same year in which the House of the Seven Gables opened for business, Salem's Essex Institute, chartered to "preserve, collect, and interpret" Essex County materials, began acquiring and restoring historic buildings. The institute purchased the seventeenth-century John Ward House and moved it from St. Peter Street to a lot behind Plummer Hall. There it would eventually be joined by a cobbler shop and the Derby Summer

The Bertram Home for Aged Men, now the John Bertram House, 29 Washington Square North. (Jim McAllister)

House. The frame of Salem's first Quaker meeting house had been moved to the property in 1860.

For the next half century, the Essex Institute led the Salem preservation movement. The museum would outbid the Society for the Preservation of New England Antiquities to purchase Samuel McIntire's Peirce-Nichols House in 1917 and would receive, as an outright gift from the Pingree family, the classic Gardner-Pingree House in 1933. The Andrew-Safford House on Washington Square West was purchased in 1947, and the Hawthorne Hotel donated the Crowninshield-Bentley House in the late 1950s. The latter was moved from its original location to a lot just east of the Gardner-Pingree House.

The city and the federal government would make important contributions to the Salem preservation movement in the second quarter of the twentieth century. For the Massachusetts tercentenary celebration in 1930, the City of Salem built Salem 1630 (later known as Pioneer Village), a re-creation of Salem as it would have appeared at the time of John Winthrop's arrival. The village, located in Forest River Park, was restored in the late 1980s. Then in 1944 the city set up a nonprofit

The Andrew Safford House, 13 Washington Square West, was purchased by the Essex Institute in 1947. (Jim McAllister)

preservation organization, Historic Salem, Inc. (HSI), to raise funds for and oversee the restoration of the home of witch trial judge Jonathan Corwin, the only building still standing in Salem with actual ties to the events of 1692. The renovations to the "Witch House" and the adjacent Bowditch House were complete by 1948. HSI turned the deeds over to the City of Salem, which continues to operate the "Witch House" as a historic attraction.

One of the most important preservation activities of the twentieth century was the establishment of the Salem Maritime National Historic Site in 1938. The site preserved for future generations the Custom House where Nathaniel Hawthorne had worked as surveyor, the home and wharf of Elias Haskett Derby, Salem's preeminent "merchant prince," and a number of other wharves and buildings dating back to Salem's heyday as a shipping port.

The 1950s started and ended on a high note for those interested in architecture and preservation. In 1951, Salem's Pickering family celebrated the three hundredth anniversary of their Broad Street home, which they had occupied since it was built. They deeded the house and property to a charitable foundation, thereby guaranteeing is preservation. And in May 1957, the Essex Institute celebrated the two hundredth anniversary of the birth of Salem's great architect and wood-carver, Samuel McIntire, by sponsoring a McIntire symposium. More than one thousand attendees toured McIntire homes and listened to talks by Abbott Lowell Cummings and other authorities on McIntire, colonial architecture, and the decorative arts.

The redevelopment era

The combination of a disruptive construction project (the Salem train depot was razed and the tracks were run underground) and the opening of North Shore Shopping Center in Peabody in the 1950s helped bring Salem's days as a major retail district to an end. Within a decade, many Salem stores had relocated to the region's hottest shopping destination or gone out of business. In 1962 Mayor Francis X. Collins appointed the Salem Redevelopment Authority (SRA) to develop an urban renewal plan that would stop the spread of blight and restore the city to its former status as one of New England's busiest retail meccas.

Against tremendous opposition from local preserva-

Under the original urban renewal plan, these Front Street buildings would have been demolished. (Jim McAllister)

tionists and others across the country, the SRA approved a plan that called for the bulldozing of a significant majority of the buildings in the 38.5-acre Heritage Plaza East Redevelopment Area, to make way for modern stores, parking and a ring road to provide better automobile access. After the plan was approved by the Massachusetts Department of Communities and Development in 1967, the demolition began. Two dozen structures, many of them built in the eighteenth and nineteenth centuries, were razed. The preservationists won a few early battles but were certainly losing the war. A case in point was the block between Church and Federal streets, now a municipal parking lot. The Victorian firehouse and Water Department building were saved, but the rest of the existing buildings on the block were torn down.

But by 1971, control of the SRA was in the hands of preservationists, most appointed by Mayor Samuel E. Zoll. Suddenly, downtown buildings were being restored, whenever possible, instead of torn down. More than four dozen pre-twentieth-century structures, including the Lyceum on Church Street, the Bowker block at the corner of New Liberty and Essex streets, and a clump of brick and brownstone Italianate buildings on Essex Street would be returned to their former glory.

During the 1970s preservation activities spread into Salem's neighborhoods. One September morning in 1971, residents of Chestnut Street, widely acknowledged as one of America's most beautiful and architecturally significant neighborhoods, woke up to find a neighbor's house being sheathed in vinyl siding. Frustrated by the lack of legal means to stop the work, the residents sprang into action. Within a few months, thanks to their efforts and the Salem city government, the Chestnut Street Historic District was established.

Other districts would be added later: Derby Street on Salem's waterfront (1974); Federal Street (1976); Washington Square, including the Salem Common and many adjacent buildings (1977); and Lafayette Street near Salem State College (1985). In 1991 the McIntire Historic District was created by combining and significantly enlarging the Chestnut and Federal Street districts.

The Ropes Mansion, 318 Essex Street. (Jim McAllister)

Exterior changes visible from a public street made to any of the nearly six hundred buildings within these districts now require a Certificate of Appropriateness from the Salem Historic District Commission. The commission later began encouraging preservation and restoration activities by making annual awards to Salem property owners.

Historic Salem, Inc., obtained a $49,890 matching grant from the National Endowment for the Arts in 1976 to inventory buildings in five of Salem's oldest neighborhoods and to develop strategies for preserving them. In the preceding decade the organization had initiated a historic house plaque program and sponsored its first biennial house and garden tour. HSI was also involved in educational programs, lobbying efforts, and other activities designed to protect and promote Salem's architectural heritage.

In 1976, the Chestnut Street Associates held its fifth "Chestnut Street Days" in as many decades as part of the American bicentennial celebration. Selected homes in the Chestnut Street neighborhood, including the museum of the Stephen Phillips Memorial Trust (established in 1971), were open to the public. Costumed residents and volunteers greeted visitors, and outdoor activities added a nineteenth-century feel to the day.

The Essex Institute, catalyst for so much preservation activity in the first half of the twentieth century, continued to do its part. It bought the Assembly House on Federal Street in 1965 and the Ropes Mansion, with its stunning formal garden, in 1989. The Institute's restoration of McIntire's Gardner-Pingree House in the mid-1980s attracted the attention of national media.

In late 1995, the eyes of America were again trained on Salem, when "This Old House," a popular PBS television show hosted by Salem's own Steve Thomas, helped restore one of the city's colonial treasures. The show was produced by Boston station WGBH and was broadcasted nationally.

The Hawthorne renaissance

Given the circumstances surrounding Nathaniel Hawthorne's departure from Salem, it was hardly surprising that he was ignored for decades by the inhabitants he left behind. But Hawthorne's image would benefit from the passage of time, as well as from the efforts of the Essex Institute, Caroline Emmerton, and others.

One of the community's first public acknowledgments of its most famous native son occurred in 1904 to commemorate the one hundredth anniversary of his birth. The celebration was organized by the Essex Institute and culminated on June 23 with "Hawthorne Day." Activities included readings from the author's works to children in Salem schools, a reception for Hawthorne family members sponsored by the Old Planters Society, and a public gathering at the Cadet Armory on Essex Street. Among the speakers at the armory was Edward Waldo Emerson, a descendant of Hawthorne's Concord neighbor Ralph Waldo Emerson. Letters were read from the American ambassador to England, Joseph Hodges Choate, and Hawthorne biographer Henry James.

A few years later, the first of many public shrines to the author's memory, the House of the Seven Gables, was opened by Caroline Emmerton. She purposely furnished the seventeenth-century house to look as it would have in Hawthorne's time, and the guided tour explored the author's relationship to the house and its owner. Later, in 1958, the museum acquired Hawthorne's birthplace on Union Street and moved it to the grounds of the House of the Seven Gables.

The restoration of the House of the Seven Gables brought national attention to both Salem and its "great romancer." The city's new appreciation of Hawthorne was summed up in a June 1925 headline in the *Salem Evening News*: "Salem Should Make the Most of the Fame of Nathaniel Hawthorne."

The Salem Hotel Corporation would reaffirm this sentiment a month later when it named its new hostelry

> Given the circumstances surrounding Nathaniel Hawthorne's departure from Salem, it was hardly surprising that he was ignored for decades.

Important Sites in Modern Salem

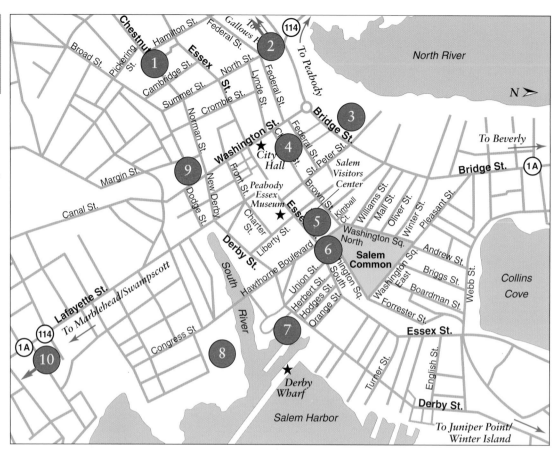

1. Chestnut Street

Originally home to some of Salem's most successful merchants, Chestnut Street is now one of America's most architecturally significant neighborhoods.

2. Blubber Hollow Located at the base of Gallows Hill, it was the center of Salem's leather business and the starting point of the great fire of 1914.

3. Site of Parker Brothers (Bridge Street) The maker of Monopoly and one of Salem's biggest employers for a century, until the factory was razed in the 1990s.

4. Salem Lyceum (43 Church Street) A focus of Salem culture since 1830, this was the site of Alexander Graham Bell's first public demonstration of the telephone.

5. Plummer Hall (132 Essex Street) Built for the Salem Athenaeum and now home to the Phillips Library of the Peabody Essex Museum.

6. Hawthorne Hotel and statue (Hawthorne Boulevard) Opened in 1925, the 89-room hotel graces Salem Common. On an adjacent mall is Bela Lyon Pratt's statue of Nathaniel Hawthorne.

7. Salem Maritime National Historic Site and Pickering Wharf In 1938, a concerted effort began to preserve historic properties on Salem's waterfront. Today the U.S. Park Service maintains the Historic Site, while Pickering Wharf (formerly Union Wharf) next door is an important private development.

8. Site of Naumkeag Mills, now Shetland Properties (Congress Street) Originally built in 1847 by the Naumkeag Steam Cotton Company and rebuilt after the fire of 1914, the complex is now an office and industrial development.

9. Site of Boston and Maine depot The railroad came to Salem in 1838, and the depot was a fixture in what is now Riley Plaza from 1848 until it was razed in the 1950s.

10. Salem State College Originally the Salem Normal School, which opened on the corner of Broad and Summer streets in 1854. The college is now located in South Salem.

on the Salem Common the Hawthorne Hotel. The author's granddaughter, Hildegarde Hawthorne, noted in a letter to the Salem Hotel Corporation, "Surely there could be no more certain indication that Salem loves and honors her famous son than this fine building of yours named for him."

While the hotel was under construction, the Hawthorne Memorial Association was busy raising the $20,000 needed to buy Bela Lyon Pratt's magnificent bronze statue of the author from the City of Boston. The life-size sculpture was placed on a grassy mall on the new Hawthorne Boulevard and was unveiled on December 23, 1925, by the author's great-granddaughter, Rosamond Mikkelsen. When the Salem Maritime National Historic Site was created in 1938, it included the Custom House where Hawthorne had worked and where he claimed, in the introduction to *The Scarlet Letter,* to have found the cloth "A" worn by Hester Prynne.

This story was very much in the public consciousness in 1938 because, just a few years earlier, the novel had been made into a film, featuring Colleen Moore in the leading role. (A later adaptation of *The Scarlet Letter* made in 1995, with Demi Moore as Hester Prynne, was less than enthusiastically received in Salem.) In 1940, *The House of the Seven Gables* was adapted for the silver screen by Twentieth Century-Fox. In a very exciting moment in Salem's popular culture, the world premier of the movie was held in the Paramount Theatre on Essex Street. A prescreening dinner was held at the House of the Seven Gables, where, the local paper reported, the

> The restoration of the House of the Seven Gables brought national attention to both Salem and its "great romancer."

"prettiest debs and past debs dressed in the costumes of the period of the Hawthorne classics." The dinner raised funds for programs at the museum's settlement house. The only damper on the excitement was the last-minute cancellation of the appearance by star Margaret Lindsay, who had taken ill.

Hollywood was rekindling interest in Nathaniel Hawthorne among movie-goers, and Manning Hawthorne was doing the same for his fellow academics. In the late 1930s and early 1940s this Hawthorne scholar and descendant allowed many Hawthorne family documents to be published by Essex Institute Historical Collections. The release of this previously unpublished material spawned five major biographies of the author. In 1962, the Ohio State University Press set out to publish a complete edition of everything that Nathaniel Hawthorne was known to have written. The last of the twenty-two volumes wasn't published until 1998.

Scholarly interest in this most intriguing and mysterious of authors led members of the Modern Language Association to found the Nathaniel Hawthorne Society in December 1974. The association's membership consists primarily of scholars and library representatives from around the world. Salem hosted the society's annual meeting in 1978 and cohosted it with Boston in 1980.

The decade beginning in 1975 would be marked by a number of important developments related to Hawthorne. A new granite fountain in Town House Square was inspired by Hawthorne's sketch "Rill From the Town Pump" (1837). On July 8, 1983, representa-

The Hawthorne Hotel. (Jim McAllister)

tives from the U.S. Postal Service were at the House of the Seven Gables to introduce a new postage stamp bearing Charles Osgood's portrait of Hawthorne. The portrait was borrowed from the Essex Institute. That same year, the institute purchased an eight-thousand-plus-piece collection of Hawthorne memorabilia from E. Fraser Clark of Michigan. Some financing for the purchase came from the sale of a rare painting of former president Andrew Jackson found in an attic at Hooper-Hathaway House on the grounds of the House of the Seven Gables.

The witch trials revisited

In a December 15, 1996, article in the *Boston Globe,* playwright Arthur Miller recalled, "I visited Salem in 1952. I thought that they still hadn't gotten over it, that they were still ashamed about it. You couldn't get anyone to say anything about it." While Miller's comment may have been a bit exaggerated, his point was well made. The Salem witch trials were such a source of guilt and shame that generations of local citizens were loath to discuss the topic at all. Evidence of this is that no one today can pinpoint the exact location of Gallows Hill, the execution site and one of the most significant landmarks in Salem history.

Town House Square fountain inspired by Nathaniel Hawthorne. (Jim McAllister)

Not everyone was afraid of the subject. Nathaniel Hawthorne, a student of colonial history and a descendant of one of the witch trial judges, made frequent use of the witch trials in his writings. A number of nineteenth-century historians helped document the story of the trials. Charles Upham, a Salem minister, historian, author, and one-time mayor, published his "Lectures on Witchcraft" in 1831. Unhappy with the final product, written at a time when he was working under "circumstances which prevented a thorough investigation of the subject," Upham later set out to chronicle in greater detail "incidents and circumstances" connected with the Salem witch trials.

This new work of more than a thousand pages, entitled *Salem Witchcraft, with An Account of Salem Village,* was published in 1867, just two years after historian W. Stanley Woodward's two-volume *Records of Salem Witchcraft.* Woodward's book compiled many Essex County legal documents relating to the trials.

In the late nineteenth century, a few local businesses took the bold step of using the witch theme for commercial purposes. One of the earliest such uses was the

The Hooper-Hathaway House, at the House of the Seven Gables. (Jim McAllister)

"Witch City" brand of fish sold by Pettingell's Fish Dealers, fixtures on Derby Wharf from approximately 1867 to 1903. In 1889, Parker Brothers published Ye Witchcraft Game, but the negative local reaction soon led the company to discontinue it. A more lasting commercial use of the witch theme was the brainchild of Salem retailer Daniel Low. In the early 1890s, Low purchased a number of souvenir spoons during a European trip. Immmediately after returning to Salem, the inspired retailer was advertising his newest product, the Salem Witch Spoon. The timing was perfect: the year was the bicentennial of the 1692 witch trials. The spoons were sold through Low's mail order catalogue, believed to be the first in the country. According to Low, this was the first souvenir spoon sold in the United States.

Salem's darkest secret was gradually brought out into the light and explored, or exploited, by commercial, academic, and cultural interests. In the 1930s, the Works Progress Administration (WPA) funded the research, compilation, and publication of all known legal documents pertaining to the witch trials. Manuscripts were collected from the Essex, Middlesex, and Suffolk County courts; the Boston Public Library and the New York Public Library; the Massachusetts State Archives, the Essex Institute, and the Massachusetts Historical Society.

The completed thirteen-hundred-page book, available to the public at the Essex Institute or Essex County Clerk of Court's office, made life much simpler for researchers. One of these was Arthur Miller, who visited the Essex Institute a number of times while researching his monumental play *The Crucible* (1953). The work drew parallels between the Salem witch trials and the witch hunt then being conducted by Senator Joseph McCarthy and the House Un-American Activities Committee. *The Crucible* has been performed at least once a day somewhere in the world since its opening on Broadway on January 22, 1958, and it has helped keep the Salem witch trials alive in the public consciousness.

> Salem's darkest secret was gradually brought out into the light and explored, or exploited.

Despite Miller's contention that the people of Salem were too ashamed of the Salem witch trials to speak of them in the 1950s, the city had already restored the "Witch House," the former residence of witch trial judge Jonathan Corwin, as an "everlasting monument to courageous men who broke the shackles of theocratic authority and paved the way for that freedom of thought which has made this country great." The public opening of the "Witch House" in May 1948 was a clear indication that Salem was willing to face the events of 1692 and to share them with visitors.

Pop culture would play an important role in promoting the connection between witches and Salem. In 1970, Elizabeth Montgomery and the cast of the popular television comedy "Bewitched" came to Salem to film two episodes to be aired during Halloween week. The episodes, jointly called the "Salem Saga," centered on a convention held to elect a new "witch in residence" for the coming year.

In a classic example of art imitating life, Salem already had a witch in residence. Laurie Cabot, a modern practitioner of the wiccan religion, had arrived in the city in the late 1960s and was on the verge of becoming a public figure at the time "Bewitched" hit Salem.

Journalists from *National Geographic, Newsweek, Time,* and other publications, not to mention film crews from television networks, descended on Salem to profile Cabot and her growing band of wiccans.

Also during the 1970s, the city's first for-profit witch attraction opened for business. The Salem Witch Museum began offering its multimedia presentation on the Salem witch trials in 1972 in the former Second Church, a Gothic Revival building on Washington Square. It would be joined by the Witch Dungeon (1979), the Salem Wax Museum of Witches and Seafarers (1993), and the Salem Witches Village (1995).

The Salem witch trials were no longer a shameful secret; they had become an engine driving the city's tourism industry. In 1982, the Salem Witch Museum organized, and ran in conjunction with the Salem Chamber of Commerce, the city's first "Haunted Happenings" Halloween festival. By the end of the century the event had grown into a three-week extravaganza featuring candlelight walks, haunted houses, psychic fairs, parades, and, to kick off the festivities, a "Fright Train" from Boston's North Station.

Serious students of the Salem witch trials did their best to keep pace with the commercial interests. The PBS television movie *Three Sovereigns for Sarah* was filmed in Danvers and the surrounding area in 1985 and featured British actress Vanessa Redgrave in the role of

Tituba gathers with other accused witches in a Salem Witch Museum tableau. (Salem Witch Museum)

Rebecca Nurse's sister Sarah Cloyce. The movie—written, produced, and directed by former area resident Victor Pisano—aired nationally on PBS stations.

Pisano's movie also helped set a serious moral tone for the upcoming commemoration of the witch trials tercentenary. In 1986, the City of Salem had appointed the Witch Trials Tercentenary Committee and charged it with developing a program of activities for 1992 that would help "lift the shroud of misunderstanding, remorse, and shame that for three centuries has been asssociated with the trials."

With the help and expertise of staff loaned from local museums, the committee coordinated events ranging from plays and school projects to a concert led by Harry Ellis Dicksen, conductor emeritus of the Boston Pops. Local professionals participated in panel discussions to examine the legal, medical, and social aspects of the trials. Other programs looked at the related themes of bigotry, hate crimes, racism, and the pursuit of tolerance and understanding. A highlight of the year was an appearance by actor Michael York, fresh from a run as John Hale in a production of *The Crucible.*

Another actor, Gregory Allen Williams, was presented with the first "Salem Award" for his heroic rescue of a truck driver who was being savagely beaten by a mob during the Los Angeles riots related to the trial of police officers accused of beating Rodney King. The presentation was made on August 5, 1992, at the dedication of the memorial to the victims of the Salem witch trials that had been erected next to the seventeenth-century Burying Point on Charter Street. The memorial had been designed by James Cutler and Maggie Smith from the state of Washington. Twenty inscribed benches memorialized the victims of the hysteria, and six locust trees (the last to bloom and first to lose their leaves) were planted to represent the stark injustice of the witch trials. The winning design was unveiled by Arthur Miller in November 1991, while noted Holocaust survivor and peace advocate Elie Wiesel served as keynote speaker at the August 1992 dedication.

"Haunted Happenings" are fun for all ages. (Jim McAllister)

Two documentary movies were produced at the time of the tercentenary. *Days of Judgment* was financed by a local corporation and produced for the Essex Institute (which would merge with the Peabody Museum in 1992 to form the Peabody Essex Museum). The film opened with a simultaneous exhibit at the museum. This exhibit featured original witch trial documents as well as paintings and artifacts related to the subject.

Witch City, a video produced by independent film-

makers, cast a critical eye on the commercialization of the Salem witch trials. The film was controversial in Salem, as might be expected, but it was viewed with interest outside of the city.

Return to the sea

None of Salem's cornerstones was so underservedly neglected as its long and illustrious maritime heritage. Sweeping the witch trials under the rug was understandable; Hawthorne's departure from Salem hardly endeared him to the local citizenry; and the razing, altering, or subdividing of many of the city's colonial homes could be rationalized in the name of providing housing. But to ignore the industry on which Salem was built was inexcusable.

But it happened. Within a few decades of the demise of the glorious East India trade, interest in matters maritime faded. By 1867, in fact, the museum of the East India Marine Society, the keeper of maritime artifacts and records from Salem's glory days, was so ignored by the general population that it was reorganized as the Peabody Academy of Science. One could still see ship models, portraits of merchants and captains, and other maritime artifacts on display, but the emphasis had switched to the natural sciences and ethnology.

Central and Derby wharves at Salem Maritime National Historic Site. (Jim McAllister)

The city turned away from the sea in the second half of the nineteenth century. Sightings of square riggers in Salem Harbor became fewer and fewer, and the shoreline was gradually turned over to industrial use. The North River, meanwhile, was overwhelmed by the leather tanning and currying shops that lined its banks and poured toxic effluent into its once-pristine waters. Both the North and South rivers would be partially filled in to make way for the railroads, new streets, and industrial and commercial development. Railroads and trolleys replaced coastal vessels as the primary mode of transportation in and out of Salem. In what may have been the unkindest cut of all, Derby Wharf, perhaps the centerpiece of Salem's maritime legacy, was sold to the Essex Street Car Railway Company at the turn of the century for the storage and repair of streetcars. Two decades earlier, another streetcar company had gobbled up a prime piece of the waterfront when it built an amusement park at Salem Willows. Salem's waterfront would hit bottom in the third quarter of the twentieth century. The New England Power Company

Reenactment, Salem Maritime National Historic Site. (Jim McAllister)

plant was built on Salem Harbor landfill by 1951 and was joined in later years by a water treatment plant and two sewage treatment plants.

But interest in Salem's maritime past and its waterfront was kept alive by a small group of citizens, institutions, and writers. The Peabody Academy of Science, which expanded its exhibition space in 1904–5, began restoring its maritime collection to former prominence. Museum publications, including the *Neptune* magazine, helped keep Salem in touch with its maritime origins and with those who shared a passion for maritime history. In 1915, the institution changed its name to the Peabody Museum.

There has never been a shortage of writers interested in the lore of the sea, and in the twentieth century many, including Ralph Paine, Samuel Eliot Morison, James Duncan Phillips, and Frank Donovan, added to the existing literature about Salem's maritime heritage. The East India Marine Society was a prolific publisher of maritime literature, and with help from its brother organization, the Salem Marine Society, it continued to maintain links between the descendants of former Salem sea captains and their "home port."

The first major step reconnecting Salem with its waterfront and maritime past was the establishment of the Salem Maritime National Historic Site by the U.S. Department of the Interior in 1938. This single event preserved and made accessible to the public the Custom House, the wharf and Georgian brick mansion of Elias Derby, an early retail shop, and a number of other eighteenth- and early-nineteenth-century buildings and wharves. For thirty years, beginning in 1947, a U.S. Navy training station, with its own submarine, was maintained on park property on Central Wharf. The removal of that training station in 1977 opened the door for more historic interpretation at the site, including the addition of two early nineteenth-century warehouses relocated from Front Street.

Another significant waterfront improvement was the building of Pickering Wharf in the late 1970s. The Pickering Coal and Oil Company sold six acres of land bordering the Salem Maritime National Historic Site to the city for half its assessed value. The subsequent development of a retail-marina-condominium-office complex on the wharf attracted residents and visitors alike. An original but short-lived attraction on the wharf was "Voyage of the India Star," an audiovisual presentation that recreated the experience of shipping out on an East Indiaman for faraway ports.

Within a few years the Pickering Wharf area had become the embarkation point for harbor tours, whale watches, and a shuttle boat to a floating restaurant in the middle of Salem Harbor. The lure of rental dock space

> Anchoring the foundation of tourism are nothing other than the cornerstones of Salem.

brought water lovers to Salem, and soon other mooring and launching facilities sprang up on the waterfront. A public launching ramp and pier were included when Winter Island, the site of Salem's earliest fishing colony and the building of the famous frigate *Essex,* was restored beginning in 1979. The lighthouses on the island and on Derby Wharf were both restored by volunteers.

In the mid-1980s the Salem Maritime National Historic Site obtained funds from the National Park Foundation for educational outreach programs. Before long, the story of Salem's great maritime heritage had been officially incorporated into the Salem school curriculum and the city's new middle school had been organized along a maritime theme. In 1986, the national park sponsored its first annual maritime festival, featuring sea chantey singers, boat-building demonstrations, and other marine activities.

In the spring and summer of 1993, the Peabody Essex Museum hosted an exhibition of some of the world's finest marine paintings from the collection of the National Maritime Museum of Greenwich England. The Salem museum was one of only three venues in the United States for the "Great Age of Sail" show, which featured paintings by J. W. Turner, Sir Joshua Reynolds, and other famous English, Dutch, and American artists.

While the "Great Age of Sail" helped to re-enforce Salem's maritime reputation, other developments in the early and mid-1990s would have a more lasting impact. Two new commercial ventures with maritime themes, the Salem Wax Museum of Witches and Seafarers and the New England Pirate Museum, opened in 1993 and

1995, respectively, and the Salem Maritime National Historic Site received $35 million in federal funds to restore its historic wharves, build a visitor center, and construct a replica of the *Friendship,* a 171-foot East Indiaman. The vessel was constructed by Scarano Boat Builders in Albany, New York, and arrived at its permanent berth on the park's Central Wharf on August 31, 1998.

Much of the impetus and support for the National Park developments came from the Salem Partnership, a coalition of representatives from the city's business, government, and nonprofit sectors. This organization was created in 1987 with a mission to undertake projects to revitalize Salem. Two of these projects are the initiation of seasonal ferry service between Boston and Salem in 1998 and aggressive marketing efforts to attract yachtsmen to the harbor.

At the millenium, Salem is a city of just over 37,000 residents. Its population includes the ethnic groups that arrived between 1840 and the Salem fire of 1914, as well as more recent immigrants from Puerto Rico, the Dominican Republic, and other Latin nations.

The city's days as a major manufacturing and retail center are over. The tanneries, with a few exceptions, and the shoe factories are gone. So are the Naumkeag Steam Cotton Mill, Sylvania, Parker Brothers, and the large retail stores that once lined busy Essex Street.

Taking their place are bed-and-breakfasts, walking trails and trolleys, a modern visitor center, new and expanded historic attractions, gift shops, and other manifestations of Salem's blooming tourism industry. That industry, anchored by all four cornerstones of the city's history, can be expected to provide a solid foundation for Salem's economy in the twenty-first century.

Mural, New England Pirate Museum. (Jim McAllister)

Looking east from Derby Wharf. (Jim McAllister)

☙ B I B L I O G R A P H Y ❧

The Maritime History of Salem

Goss, K. David. *Salem: Maritime Salem in the Age of Sail*. Washington: U.S. National Park Service, 1987.

Peabody, Robert E. *Merchant Ventures of Old Salem*. Boston: Houghton Mifflin, 1912.

Phillips, James D. *Salem and the Indies*. Boston: Houghton-Mifflin, 1947.

———. *Salem in the Seventeenth Century*. Boston: Houghton-Mifflin, 1933.

———. *Salem in the Eighteenth Century*. Reprinted, Salem: Essex Institute, 1969.

The Witchcraft Trials of 1692

Boyer, Paul, and Stephen Nissenbaum. *Salem Possessed: The Social Origins of Witchcraft*. Cambridge, MA: Harvard University Press, 1974.

Hansen, Chadwick. *Witchcraft at Salem*. New York: George Braziller, 1969.

Hoffer, Peter Charles. *The Devil's Disciples: Makers of the Salem Witchcraft Trials*. Baltimore, MD: The Johns Hopkins University Press, 1996.

Roach, Marilynne K. *In the Days of the Salem Witchcraft Trials*. Boston: Houghton Mifflin, 1996.

Rosenthal, Bernard. *Salem Story: Reading the Witch Trials of 1692*. Cambridge, UK: Cambridge University Press, 1993.

Starkey, Marion L. *The Devil in Massachusetts*. New York: Knopf, 1949.

Trask, Richard B. *The Devil Hath Been Raised: A Documentary History of the Salem Village Witchcraft Outbreak of March 1692*. Danvers, MA: Yeoman Press, 1997.

Upham, Charles W. *Salem Witchcraft*. 2 volumes. Frederick Ungar Publishing, 1969 (originally published in 1867).

Architecture of Historic Salem

Cousins, Frank, and Phil M. Riley. *The Colonial Architecture of Salem*. Boston: Little, Brown & Co., 1919.

Cousins, Frank, and Phil M. Riley. *The Wood-Carver of Salem: Samuel McIntire, His Life and His Work*. Boston: Little Brown & Co., 1916. Reprinted, New York: AMS Press, Inc., 1970.

Cummings, Abbott Lowell. *The Framed Houses of Massachusetts Bay, 1625-1725*. Cambridge and London: Belknap Press of the Harvard University Press, 1979.

Farnam, Ann, and Bryant F. Tolles, Jr., eds. *The Essex Institute Historic House Booklet Series*. Salem: Essex Institute, 1976-78. Booklets on the John Ward, Crowninshield-Bentley, Peirce-Nichols, Assembly, Gardner-Pingree, Andrew-Safford and John Tucker Daland houses.

Kimball, Fiske. *Mr. Samuel McIntire, Carver: The Architect of Salem*. Salem: Essex Institute, 1940. Reprinted, Gloucester, MA: Peter Smith, 1964.

Labaree, Benjamin W., ed. *Samuel McIntire: A Bicentennial Symposium, 1757-1957*. Salem: Essex Institute, 1957.

Norton, Paul F. "Samuel McIntire," from Adolf K. Plazek, ed., *Macmillan Encyclopedia of Architects* 3. New York: The Free Press, 1982.

Tolles, Bryant F., Jr. *Architecture in Salem: An Illustrated Guide*. Salem: Essex Institute, 1983.

Tolles, Bryant F., Jr. "Salem," from Jane Turner, ed., *The Dictionary of Art* 27. New York: Grove Dictionaries, Inc., 1996.

Nathaniel Hawthorne

Hawthorne, Nathaniel. *Novels*. New York: The Library of America, 1983. (Includes all five of Hawthorne's longer romances)

_____. *Tales and Sketches*. New York: The Library of America, 1982. (Includes the complete tales and sketches, plus the children's stories of *The Wonder Book* and *Tanglewood Tales*)

Erlich, Gloria C. *Family Themes and Hawthorne's Fiction: The Tenacious Web*. New Brunswick, NJ: Rutgers, 1984.

Gollin, Rita. *Portraits of Nathaniel Hawthorne: An Iconography*. Dekalb: Northern Illinois University Press, 1983.

Loggins, Vernon. *The Hawthornes: The Story of Seven Generations of an American Family*. New York: Columbia University Press, 1951.

Mellow, James R. *Nathaniel Hawthorne in His Times*. Boston: Houghton Mifflin, 1980.

Miller, Edwin Haviland. *Salem Is My Dwelling Place: A Life of Nathaniel Hawthorne*. Iowa City: University of Iowa Press, 1991.

Moore, Margaret B. *The Salem World of Nathaniel Hawthorne*. Columbia: University of Missouri Press, 1998.

Turner, Arlin. *Nathaniel Hawthorne: A Biography*. New York: Oxford University Press, 1980.

Salem Then and Now

Robotti, Frances Diane. *Chronicles of Old Salem*. Salem: Newcomb and Gauss, 1948.

Winwar, Frances. *Puritan City*. New York: National Travel Club, 1938.

Batchelder, H. M. and Charles Osgood. *An Historical Sketch of Salem 1626–1879*. Salem: Essex Institute, 1879. (Reprinted, Salem: Higginson Books.)

Hurd, D. Hamilton, *History of Salem*. Philadelphia: J. W. Lewis and Company, 1888. (Reprinted, Salem: Higginson Books.)

Bedford, Faith Andrews. *Frank W. Benson, American Impressionist*. New York: Rizzoli, 1994.